INTERIORS OF A STORYTELLER

INTERIORS OF A STORYTELLER

STEPHANIE SABBE

FOREWORD BY HOLLY WILLIAMS

PHOTOGRAPHS BY JOSEPH BRADSHAW

Gibbs Smith

To my children. Being your mama
is all I have ever really wanted to be.
Bryan, being your wife is pretty
great as well.

First Edition
29 28 27 26 25   5 4 3 2

Text © 2025 Stephanie Sabbe
Foreword © 2025 Holly Williams
Photographs © 2025 Joseph Bradshaw
Watercolor Portraits © 2025 Oxonoo
House Illustrations © 2025 Tauseef Ahmed

Published by
Gibbs Smith
570 N. Sportsplex Dr.
Kaysville, Utah 84037

1.800.835.4993 orders
www.gibbs-smith.com

Designed by Sheryl Dickert
Printed and bound in China
This product is made of FSC®-certified and other controlled material.

Library of Congress Cataloging-in-Publication Data: 2024943043
ISBN: 978-1-4236-6764-3

CONTENTS

FOREWORD

What is the thing I love most about this lovely book that you are about to delve into? Stephanie has repeatedly said she wrote it for her children—her littles will always be able to reach out and open up these pages. If it is not a success in the literal sense (which is highly doubtful), it will always be, no matter what, the biggest success to her precious family, because don't we all want to soak in the written stories of those who first loved us?

In these stunning pages, they will not only witness the obvious talent of their incredible mama, but more importantly, they will see her heart, which shines ever so brightly here. They will ooh and aah over the absolutely stunning interiors—a room for every occasion—since she is truly one of the greats when it comes to her work passion: interior design. But the stories—oh, the stories. They are so richly woven together—word by word, project by project, year by year—toward the beautiful, sad, hilarious, intriguing, and downright incredible finales.

The funny thing is, I haven't spent much time with Stephanie in person. We have had one lunch and a few hang times together, which I could count on one hand. But I've spent a lot of time with her words, her heart, and her talent through her social media channels. She is a girls' girl, a mother for the ages, a deeply kind soul, a poet, and to top it all off, one of the funniest people around. Her work will stand the test of time, no question. You will see a kitchen, a bedroom, or a child's room and have absolutely no idea what decade it was created. That is what the greats do: you can't tell when their work was completed because it is so timeless, so classic, so evergreen. *Warmth* is the first word that comes to mind when I think of her interiors—there is nothing cold or stark or overly minimal. Her use of color, of classic hardware finishes, of scale, and of perfect fabric choices is enveloping in each of her rooms. When I look at them, I feel like a lovely cashmere blanket is being draped over my senses; she is just that good.

She has a beautiful and very busy life with four adoring children and a superstar husband who is saving lives every single day in the medical field. For those of us in the overwhelming parenting stage, it is easy to get caught in the relentless cycle and never break from it, but I am so thankful she found the margin and dug deep to complete this book. And you will be also. Whether you are in the most grinding season of your career or at home slicing apples for lunch and chasing little feet, there is something for all of us in these pages ahead. And that, my friends, is a true work of art . . .

—HOLLY WILLIAMS

*SINGER-SONGWRITER, RETAIL ENTREPRENEUR, SERIAL
HOUSE RENOVATOR, AND LOVER OF THE SOUTH*

CHAPTER 1

FROM STALLONE TO
ALONE (IN A TREE)

I was born in 1981 in Huntington, West Virginia. At the time, my father worked for the local power company and my mom was an administrative assistant at nearby Marshall University. Despite living just shy of middle class, I believed with my whole heart that we were probably rich. We had an above-ground pool behind our one-level brick house. Prior to that brick house, we'd lived in a mobile home where my nursery was decorated in a Bambi theme. My mother loved a Walmart bed-in-a bag or any sort of pre-curated matching set, once declaring to my adult self, "They would not make the wallpaper border if we were not supposed to use it." She also loved red sports cars, cold Bud Light, and winning any and all arguments. I never knew my dad's drink of choice, which says a lot to how little I knew about my dad. But he spent over thirty years in AA, where I've heard step 9 is to "make amends." I have no personal recollection of amends being made to me, so I'm guessing he also had a knack, like my mother, for never being wrong.

Shortly after we moved into our brick ranch home, my mom upgraded me to a Strawberry Shortcake–themed big-girl room, gave birth to my brother Brennan, and then separated from my dad for the first of many times. Or maybe he left her. Details again that no one ever made clear. I blamed Sylvester Stallone. You see, my mom went on a work trip to Acapulco that year and Sylvester Stallone happened to be filming a movie there at the time. She and her friends attended an event where they got to take a picture with Sly himself. When a photo of him and my mom showed up on her nightstand inside a beach-themed frame, my dad was suddenly out of the picture. Naturally I concluded this overly muscular man in a tank top was going to be my new stepdad.

My parents officially filed for divorce when I was five. My mom rented a two-bedroom apartment close to the Nashville fairgrounds, and I attended the nearby public school. One afternoon I came home from kindergarten in a panic. Our assignment was to memorize our home phone number. My teacher sent me home with a note, and my mom wrote back to confirm: "She is correct, we cannot currently afford to have a home phone line." No one ever discussed being poor with me. No one ever discussed much at all with me or my little brother. We were just sort of two small witnesses to what appeared to be our parents' lives unraveling. That same year, my mom brought me along to a confrontation with my dad and his new girlfriend in the parking lot of an AA meeting. With no money for a phone, we definitely didn't have money for a babysitter. She screamed at the woman as the new couple jogged to the car and slammed the doors shut. Me just standing awkwardly behind the bumper of our car, twirling the ends of my hair—*Hey, Dad!* My mom celebrated my dad's newfound freedom and even newer romantic relationship by repeatedly kicking the passenger door like a WWF fighter until the car sped away. I quickly skirted over and buckled myself into the front seat of our car, terrified as my mom cried and beat the steering wheel. "Where," I wondered, "is my new fricking stepdad and his big muscles when we really need him?"

We moved into a condo complex in a neighboring part of town the following year. The public schools were better in Bellevue and we could afford a phone line. Things were looking up! I was so proud of our new living situation that I drew endless pictures of our two-story condo while sitting in my first-grade class. The buildings were light blue with a dark blue trim. There was a pool and even a gazebo where we could wait for the school bus completely unsupervised, as was standard practice in the mid-'80s. I learned more about life sitting at that bus stop with those older kids than anywhere I have hung out since. But the condo complex was a lovely place to live for a single mom and two little kids. My teacher had us draw ourselves in front of our homes so she could turn them into melamine plates for Mother's Day gifts. Feeling already above the curve on this particular assignment, I drew myself wearing a huge smile, standing in front of our blue condo, every window detailed, with flowers lining the walkway. My mom kept her plate on display in our kitchen well into my adulthood, once proudly reminding me, "You drew this the year we got divorced. See how you are smiling? You were happy!" I thought to myself, "Wow, I have been at this for a long time." No one ever asked me, but that smile was most definitely not an accurate depiction of my internal state at that time. But the plate was a gift—including the smile—the smile of a little girl embarking on a lifelong journey of feeling responsible for her mother's happiness. Decades later I learned the term *enmeshment*—if enmeshment were an Olympic sport, I would win the gold medal, no doubt. But being creative was an escape for me even then. When I lost myself in creativity, I didn't have to think about the harder things life threw my way. I cannot remember a time when I didn't dream and daydream about design. Sometimes I think that without design, I would probably be insane.

I was ten years old, sitting high in a tree near the condo's communal mailboxes, when I spotted workers installing siding over the original vertical, painted cedar. Squinting from my perch, I realized with horror that the siding was vinyl. I was a latchkey kid with holes in my shoes who ate Kid Cuisine for dinner most nights, but

I sat back with my arms folded in full contempt as if I were the eighty-five-year-old president of the local architectural historical society whispering, "There goes the neighborhood!" Our class had taken a field trip to historic Travelers Rest, and I'd even constructed a replica of the Plantation from sugar cubes. (It would later be the site of my wedding reception.) I didn't see any vinyl siding over there! I get that this is mildly offensive as vinyl siding is still prevalent in much of the United States, but cut me a little slack—fretting over questionable siding choices was a distraction from other more life-altering situations going on at the time.

These days, people throw up expensive homes faster than you can say "Whoa! They tore that house down overnight!" Modest stone cottages that once lined the streets in Nashville are being gradually replaced by what we unaffectionately refer to as "tall-skinnies." Rather than restore aging homes, builders led by private equity groups scrape existing lots to build two homes for the price of one. I've seen it more times than I care to count. There is usually an initial outcry from the neighborhood at the loss of the original home's history and character. (Hello, ten-year-old me sitting high in my tree; and hello, forty-two-year-old me sitting high in my minivan posting snarky comments on Instagram.) But when those new tall-skinnies eventually sell, the outrage subsides and it's back to business as usual. Life goes on, until the next cottage falls.

A couple of summers ago, I drove back to our old brick house in Huntington, West Virginia—the home of my Strawberry Shortcake bedroom. It had been thirty-seven years since my last visit, but the house looked exactly as I remembered, minus the handprints—mine and my brother's—pressed into the original concrete driveway. That had been repaved. I snuck around back to see if the pool was still there and, to my absolute shock, it was. Although for anyone who's spent any time in southern West Virginia, that may not shock at all. A fair amount of people tend to hang on to things there—large appliances, broken-down cars, and apparently dilapidated swimming pools—often in their yards. When a neighbor came out to do his next-door-neighbor duties of interrogating the trespasser, I introduced myself. He nodded approvingly. He said he knew exactly who I was. He'd built his house alongside my dad. They'd laid the brick themselves, he said, side by side. I do not have a lot of memories of my parents being happily married, so recalling them building things instead of breaking them was such a treat. Both houses looked as good as the day they were built. Which got me to wondering, in the midst of my weird family-history discussion with this complete stranger, "When did we stop building things intended to last?" My parents were absolutely not living in abundance in 1979. Their marriage, as previously mentioned, did not stand the test of time. Yet unlike so many newly constructed homes these days, the home they built did exactly that. As a heavily therapized adult, I still carry around a lot of unintended shame for many of the things my very young parents exposed me to while they were on their own often-tumultuous journey to figure out life. But in that moment, standing in that yard, I was so very proud of the two people who brought both me and that sturdy brick house into this world.

LEIPERS FORK

A lesson I learned in childhood: the way you start does not have to dictate how you finish. Our Leipers Fork project is a prime example. An adorable little historic town thirty minutes south of Nashville, Leipers Fork was settled in the 1700s and is home to some of the most charming shops and restaurants in our corner of the South. Surrounding the tiny downtown are large plots of farmland, making it a popular destination for families looking to step away from bustling city life. This was the case for Jordan and Brad Huggins, who in 2020 began planning to relocate their family of four from Boston to the Nashville area. The project began in a very atypical way for our firm. Our friend Lauren called to say she had been working with a client to select finishes for a spec house. Due to unforeseeable circumstances, she was not going to be able to help them finish the project. Lauren thought our firm's default style, along with our background with work in New England, would align well with the Huggins' vision. She reached out to see if we may have the bandwidth to jump in. We took the project under the assumption that we would purely be furnishing a new home. Little did we know our role would snowball into something much more involved than simply selecting sofas and rugs.

Spec houses are strange beasts that I did not fully understand until taking on this project. Our experience lies more in custom and renovation work. The home was presold prior to completion, most definitely as a result of an unknown market amid the COVID quarantine. Our clients were told they could select their finishes, plumbing fixtures, cabinetry, and lighting. When the contractor realized he had inadvertently gotten himself into building a custom home, he went dark—he completely cut off communication and finished the project how he wanted. Unapologetically he apparently offered our clients the opportunity to walk away. That is when I realized how crazy the spec-house world can be. But in the time between the accepted offer and the close date, the home had already greatly appreciated—a surprising twist of COVID's effect on the real estate world. Our clients chose to not walk away. They instead took on the enormous task of making changes post-construction completion to get the home they thought they had agreed upon in the first place. And if you're wondering, "How could the contractor do that!?" I have no clue. Maybe the customization was all a gentleman's agreement? But just know that he can and he did. But here's the secret: people hire and work with an architect directly if they are building a custom home. Otherwise, if it's builder led and you've never met the architect, it's most likely a spec house.

My friend Catherine Sloan, a local architect known for her gift of creating "new-old homes," had drawn the original plans. We worked with that set to instruct our game plan on getting this home to resemble her initial design. We ripped out the modern fireplace surrounds and poorly designed cabinetry. We painted, wallpapered, and did everything we could come up with to take this all-white, drywall box of an interior to the charming, New England–inspired country home our clients had dreamed of. We pulled together vivid patterns and rich textures, sourced vintage rugs and antique furniture—all to give this standard-issue space a one-of-a-kind story. The muted blue in the foyer wraps upstairs into the playroom, where we created a stage-like niche complete with operable curtains for the two young boys to put on shows for their parents. I always pride myself on being very involved with the architectural interiors of a project and this project made me realize that magic can be had without tearing the whole house apart. From the alternating-stripes sofa in the family room, to the velvet canopy bed in the primary bedroom, to the circus-inspired toile in the dining room, the home is truly a visual feast. It's not the house my clients initially thought they were purchasing. There are no interior transom windows, no paneling along the walls. The handrail to the stairs looks to be from a much more contemporary home. But through some fairly noninvasive tweaks (the fireplaces absolutely had to go), it's an escape from the city where the Jordan grows dahlias and the children perform plays. It's not the house they thought they were getting, but in so many better ways, it's the house they now happily call home.

ABOVE: A testament to the power of color. Benjamin Moore's Essex Green in a high gloss along with the more subdued Water's Edge completely transform this previously white, sterile spec-house space into something out of historic New England brownstone.

RIGHT: Pattern upon pattern, this space is a visual feast.

FOLLOWING SPREAD: This cozy sunroom wears many hats: play space, yoga studio, game room, and more.

Between the checkerboard tile, Scalamandre wallpaper, and antique barristers, we quite literally threw the kitchen sink at this one.

We often design breakfast banquets when creating homes for growing families. Always room for one more!

ABOVE: The antique mirror over the new Highland House buffet creates the perfect juxtaposition we strove for when designing this home.

RIGHT: As a native southerner, a good toile will always feel like home to me. This circus pattern by Kravet added just the right touch of kitsch to this otherwise formal space.

FOLLOWING SPREAD: The painting by Meghean Warner really made the space what it is. The alternating Guy Goodfellow striped sofa was a close second.

ABOVE: We love creating pause moments like this throughout a home—Something to give your eyes a break from the visual chaos of the more heavy-duty function spaces.

RIGHT: People always ask me when assembling a budget: "What would you spend your money on?" Cabinets. Every time, good inset cabinets.

What our client craved most was character, and character we brought.

Guest rooms should feel special, like a big hug from a friend that will stay with you long after your visit. This little pattern-heavy space checks all the boxes.

Designing children's spaces is such a treat, like getting to play on the playground again well after you have exceeded the height restriction.

Let's be honest, nurseries are for the parents. Babies have no idea where they are. And one day, this baby will beg to stick Paw Patrol stickers all over this grasscloth. But until then, may they rock peacefully in a room completely free of cartoon dogs working as public servants.

CHAPTER 2

THE DAUGHTER OF
A SEXY DEVIL

I tell the story of how I became an interior designer so often that I am positive it is scarring my children, who can basically recite it by heart. They have yet to solidify their career plans, but at twelve, ten, eight, and six, they have a little time, I suppose. I, on the other hand, a late bloomer in all other categories of life (still waiting on boobs), was the earliest of bloomers when it came to deciding a career path. I was in the second grade at West Meade Elementary in Nashville at the annual school carnival. A fortune teller (read a teacher dressed as a fortune teller) gazed into her crystal ball (a discarded flush-mount light fixture) and pronounced mysteriously, "You, Stephanie Frye, will be an interior designer when you grow up!" This was a new idea. I pondered aloud, "What exactly do they do?" She said something about curtains and pillows, but when I pressed her for more, anxiously aware that the line behind me was getting longer, she threw out a few more details. I considered for another moment, declared

"Sounds good," then skipped over to join my younger brother at the dunking booth. Quick and confident decisions have always been a strong suit of mine. Now it was settled. My career path had been established.

In fourth grade, I added an addendum to my life plan. I wanted to be an interior designer and a Christian. I believe that God came to earth in the form of a person named Jesus. This Jesus bore the burden of my already countless sins—and the many more to come (I was only nine)—so I could be forgiven by God and at peace with myself. Thirty-three years later, I'm still designing and still believing.

Though it's true that I grew up "in church," honestly, that paints an image, particularly in the South, of smocked dresses and families at church potlucks. That doesn't depict my experience. My mom chose our tiny "Free Will Southern Baptist Church" based almost entirely on its architectural resemblance to the one-room church in her small West Virginia hometown. The day she decided that we would attend church, which up to then had been limited to Easter Sundays and the occasional Christmas concert, she dropped off my brother and me at the front door before Sunday school, only to return when the main service had adjourned, rolling up fifteen minutes late in her two-door rusted red Camaro, with a little mascara on her face from the night before. She reminded us ever so often that being a single mom of two kids was not her life plan and by god she was not going to let that stop her from enjoying the occasional night out with fellow divorcées at the local honky-tonks. As a now forty-two-year-old mother of four, I don't blame her one bit. Dropping us off at church on Sunday might have been her atonement for whatever went down the night before. Or perhaps she wanted better for us than she wanted for herself.

Either way, what could go wrong?

Answer: all kinds of things. That first Sunday my brother and I pronounced Job *job*, we confessed that we didn't own a single Bible and, worse, we revealed that we usually grocery-shopped on Sundays. (At this there were audible gasps.) Our mother was young, smokin' hot, and divorced—a triple threat to the '80s Southern Baptist status quo church scene. We did not exactly fit in. The pastor once built an entire sermon around the evils of R-rated movies. I did not blink the entire sermon as my sweaty hands clutched the pew cushion for dear life, fearing somehow he knew we'd seen *Top Gun* in the theater earlier that week. Always ready to expunge myself from any pent-up guilt, I wanted to raise my hand to assure the congregation, "Don't worry about us, everyone! Our mom totally covered our eyes for the sex scenes! We only heard the noises." On another occasion, I showed up to a church "costume party" (Halloween was for the "unsaved") dressed as a man. Full beard, bald wig, suit, tie, top hat—the whole shebang. My mom—also a very creative person—really excelled at Halloween. My gender-creative (is that a term!?) costume could only have been more jarring to that mostly homeschooled crew if I had dressed as the devil himself. I bobbed for apples with peers dressed as their American Girl dolls, my little beard hairs floating about in the aluminum tub. Meanwhile, my mom was at home putting the finishing touches on her sexy devil costume for the actual Halloween festivities we'd be partaking in later that week. After spending hours that night removing the fake-beard hair, I decided to trade my old man costume for a clown for our neighborhood's round-two celebration. Aside from the architecture, why my mother chose a Free Will Baptist Church, I will honestly never know.

In spite of it all, I became a Christian of my own free will after collecting a bit of information and very much kept it to myself throughout most of my adolescence. It resonated with me when I heard about how God is a father to the fatherless (me!) and that Jesus chose to hang out with a bunch of societal rejects (also me!). After all, I spent a good deal of my childhood sipping Shirley Temples in smoky karaoke bars with a crew of divorcées, so none of it was a very hard sell. But I was confident early on that I was probably not going to pursue my faith in the same way as those adults of that old Southern Baptist church. I loved Jesus, and I was and am so thankful they introduced me to him. But I also loved the ragtag crew my mom raised us around. Jesus was not counting Bibles, so neither would I. I just wanted to be born-again.

The Presbyterians call it sanctification. But the Baptists call it being "born again." I know it's a little creepy/cultish sounding, but what's not appealing about an infinite number of do-overs? It's the concept of grace and why I love mornings, Mondays, and January firsts.

Decades later, I sat in an airplane headed for Las Vegas reading every last word of a book I had picked up called *Blue Like Jazz*, by Donald Miller. The book talked about smoking cigarettes and eating chocolate while reading the Bible, which barely cracks the surface of what it was really about. But fifteen years later, that's what still sticks with me. It felt scandalous at the time, which only made me love it more. All of a sudden I was questioning, "Was faith more than a list of rules? More than good versus evil? What does it even mean to be good?" Don wrote, "Believing in God is as much like falling in love as it is a decision. Love is both something that happens to you and something you decide upon." I was so intrigued I bought a ticket to hear this controversial author speak and stood in line to have him autograph my book.

It felt like one of those crazy, coincidental (or perhaps God-ordained) moments in life when thirteen years later, my phone rang. The caller introduced herself as a personal assistant. She said, "I am calling on behalf of Donald and Betsy Miller. They would like to interview you for a couple of upcoming projects they're working on in Nashville, if you are interested." Don now owns a very successful business consulting company called Storybrand. It's been a decade and then some since he wrote *Blue Like Jazz*, but I try to refer to the book at least once every meeting, even though his assistant, Carey, has multiple times tried to usher me away from the topic. That book, in the moment in which I read it, (coincidentally around the time my church pastor was outed for fraud,) changed my perspective on organized religion. It affirmed my belief that God is bigger than counting Bibles and grocery-shopping on Sundays. That book carved a place at the table for the eight-year-old little girl dressed as a fifty-eight-year-old man, a place for the fatherless daughter of a sexy devil.

world. My life testifies to this because I care more about my food and shelter and happiness than about anybody else.

I am learning to believe better things. I am learning to believe that other people exist, that fashion is not truth; rather, Jesus is the most important figure in history, and the gospel is the most powerful force in the universe. I am learning not to be passionate about empty things, but to cultivate passion for justice, grace, truth, and communicate the idea that Jesus likes people and even loves them.

112

(11)

Confession

Coming Out of the Closet

WHEN I WAS IN SUNDAY SCHOOL AS A KID, MY teacher put a big poster on the wall that was shaped in a circle like a target. She had us write names of people we knew who weren't Christians on little pieces of paper, and she pinned the names to the outer circle of the target. She said our goal, by the end of the year, was to move those names from the outer ring of the circle, which represented their distance from knowing Jesus, to the inner ring, which represented them having come into a relationship with Jesus. I thought the strategy was beautiful because it gave us a goal, a visual.

I didn't know any people who weren't Christians, but I was a child with a fertile imagination so I made up some names; Thad Thatcher was one and William Wonka was another. My teacher didn't believe me which I took as an insult, but nonetheless, the class was excited the very next week when both Thad and William had become Christians in a dramatic conversion experience that included the dismantling of a large satanic cult and underground drug ring. There was also levitation involved.

Even though they didn't exist, Thad and William were the only

113

THE CARRIAGE HOUSE

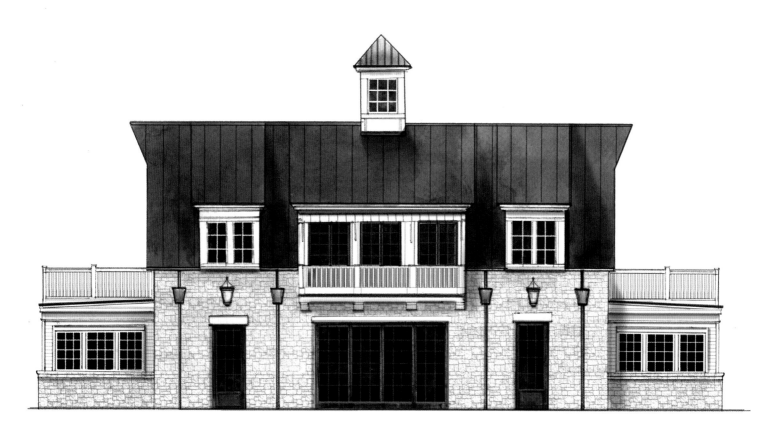

The Carriage House, a structure designed to host events and meetings, was my first project for the Millers. When I joined the team, construction was already in full swing. They had hired local architect Preston Shea; and for the interiors, the Millers had originally worked with a designer who was based out of the country and decided in the throes of COVID that having someone local would be a better fit. The hammers were already swinging before I arrived. The construction superintendent, Nathan, was five years into working on the Millers' nine-acre property named Goose Hill, which began with the construction of their main house, designed by Preston and Paris-based interior designer Kathryn Ivey. Nathan's eagerness for the project helped so much to quickly get my bearings. During our initial interview, Don had mentioned loving the interiors of Soho House Chicago. Soho House is a private social club network with locations all over the world. The Chicago location was originally built in 1908 as a belt factory. Needless to say, we were not working with the same level of charm and patina in this freshly constructed space. The original design for the Carriage House had a drywall ceiling with a grid of recessed can lights. During our first construction meeting, I asked Nathan if he thought the Millers would let me rip out the newly constructed ceiling and replace it with something with more character. He said, "I think so. Just ask." So I did, and the Millers said yes. From there I felt like all creativity blockers were dissolved and I was ready to do my best work. When I joined the project, HVAC ducts that run the length of the main space on each side of the first floor had been wrapped in drywall, and they just looked like, well, HVAC ducts. I came up with an idea to skim-coat them in concrete and add score lines. We built vertical boxed columns and applied the same treatment. The University of Tennessee School of Architecture, my alma mater, is housed in a reinforced concrete structure, which is basically steel embedded into concrete. When constructing this type of building, the concrete cures and the forms used to hold the shape are bent and snapped, leaving a grid of tie holes remaining. I spent years of college staring at these tie holes during class, thinking they looked like someone's thumbprint. And so twenty years later, when looking to create that same aesthetic, I used just that—the subs thumbprints! They all thought it was hilarious and so much fun. I was even more elated just having been given the opportunity to design something so unique and out of the box.

We lit the ceiling with floating glass globes we had shipped from England, and we tiled the kitchen (floor to ceiling) in an M. C. Escher–inspired tessellation pattern. We left the concrete floors exposed and lined the walls with floor-to-ceiling books. Famed furniture maker Grant Trick helped us with the custom upholstered grape-colored chaises as well as the U-shaped wingback sectional. I hand-drew the concept for the Cox London chandelier in the flex space; through their unequivocal craftsmanship and attention to detail, it hangs as more of a piece of art than a lighting fixture. Every little piece tells a story all its own. Recently, the Millers allowed me to throw one of my dearest friends a fortieth birthday party in the Carriage House. I received a text thirty minutes before the party, asking, "Is this space heated? Do I need to bring a big coat? " We ate, drank, and danced under the dimly lit frosted globes. Being able to use a space I designed for a personal party was such a one-of-a-kind, special experience. The next day I hilariously received a follow-up text from the same friend: "I cannot believe I asked you if that space was heated." Yes, the Carriage House is heated and cooled and so, so much more.

ABOVE: This chandelier by Cox London is the sixth love of my life following my husband and children. Every time I am in this space, I just stare at it.

RIGHT: I found this tapestry on Etsy after designing this space, and I had it framed locally. It is so perfect for the space that it appears as though it was the inspiration for the entire design.

FOLLOWING SPREAD: Used as a meeting room for our client's company as well as private event venue, this space made my inner creative self come alive in a way I had yet to ever experience. Thank you, Millers.

As a child, I used to stare with wonder at M. C. Escher books. When I presented this space, that is exactly how I described it: "Behold, an M. C. Escher kitchen." I did magician arms and everything.

YOLO ("you only live once," for those of you not up to date with the cool-kid slang like myself) applies to your metal finishes as well.

LEFT: I collected this wall of portraits over time and hung them here as a nod to the uniqueness of each person's individual story. My client's company is called Storybrand. Nailed it.

ABOVE: Something old—the antique campaign chest. Something new—the Woodville table lamp made of cast brass and then bronzed to perfection.

ABOVE: While designing this space, my client and his wife had their first child. The husband requested a space where the baby could nap while he worked, and I recall bursting his bubble with my real-world street smarts on how babies actually work.

RIGHT: Our client was not a fan of photography, which is typically a default for me when sourcing masculine art. I had this piece commissioned by Wellon Bridgers. It gives the room just the bit of softness and variation it needed.

LEFT: I found this antique piece at one of my Nashville favorites, Patina and Co.

ABOVE: The Natasha Baradaran fabric we used on this sofa is on repeat in our office. But we peaked when we paired it with this tonal velvet piping.

Finding unique antique mirrors for bathrooms has been a favorite mission for me over the years. I try my hardest to never specify an off-the-shelf mirror. Why would you, when there are so many gems out there just waiting to be found?

CHAPTER 3

HIGH ATOP THE HOLLER

My mom sent my younger brother Brennan and I to stay with our grandmother for the summer during a couple of our elementary grade-school years. My grandmother, Georgia Adkins, my daughter's namesake, was a woman of few words who raised her eight children deep in the "holler" of a town called Harts Creek, West Virginia. My mother was prone to unpredictable mood swings, which at its worst went from raging anger to shutting herself in her bedroom for days at a time. But my grandmother was anything but unpredictable. She was up with the chickens and her first pot of coffee every morning. Our summers with her made for some of my absolute best childhood memories. Having moved to Nashville when I was four years old, I was a bit culturally removed from this part of my family, but as soon as my mom's red Mercury Cougar hit that dirt road, I felt a sense of homecoming. These were my people. A literal parade of aunts and uncles stood on their porches as cousins flew out the door to chase our car as my mom cautiously navigated a road not intended for a two-wheel-drive vehicle. The last challenge was always traversing a small bridge, constructed of mud and railroad ties, that crossed the creek. The prize at the end was my Grandma Georgie. Five foot four, with permed brown hair, thick yellow-tinted eyeglasses, and a button-down flannel shirt regardless of the season—there she stood on her cinder-block front porch, with an orange-tinted bug light illuminating her face, arms wide, waiting with a kiss on the lips. Always a kiss on the lips.

Once settled in, we beelined down the holler—or was it *up* the holler? I could never keep those two straight. My uncles of all ages—and there were many—mockingly shook their heads when I got it wrong, muttering, "You city people." You have never known a sense of pride of origin until you get to know a multigenerational clan living in the mountains of Appalachia. We spent those summers swinging on grapevines, picking wild blueberries, and hunting for prehistoric writings in caves. We woke with the rooster crow as my grandmother, always up first, sipped her coffee and smoked her cigarette. After a bowl of Raisin Bran and an episode of *The Price Is Right*, we were out the door, only to return when the lightning bugs started to glow.

One summer, my older cousin Toboy (his birth certificate says Elbert; I honestly have no clue on the origins of Toboy) had just graduated from high school and was staying in the holler with my grandmother as well. Somehow we convinced him to build us a treehouse. We scoured yards and sheds, digging through scrap piles on various family members' property until we had all we needed. We'd lived in a condo complex in Nashville with no sort of claim to any outdoor space, so having a tree that we were allowed to nail wood to, not to mention the burbling creek filled with crawdads below, felt like the greatest luxury of all time. The tree itself forked at the top, and my cousin Toboy came up with a sort of trapezoidal floor plan that allowed it to anchor at three points. There was no porch and no ladder—we climbed a knotted rope to the top and entered through a hatch door in the roof. Toboy also built a dock-like landing on the bank below that allowed us to use that knotted rope to swing back and forth, bank to dock, dock to bank, over and over for hours on end, strands of the tattered rope dripping as it grazed the muddy water below. The treehouse looked like Dolly Parton's coat of many colors—some boards painted, some more rotted than others—but it was my first foray into design *and* construction, and I was hooked. I recalled adults saying you can't buy happiness, but as I lay atop our magnificent, windowless trapezoid, I thought, "Maybe not, but you sure can build it."

My brother Brennan had broken his foot playing baseball shortly before our departure from Nashville and was unable to participate in some of the more physically challenging activities that summer. That included climbing the rope to the top of the treehouse. My brother and I were only fourteen months apart, and we spent what felt like every second of our lives side by side, including sharing a bedroom back in Nashville. So being able to sneak away and enjoy this freshly constructed space alone was the cherry on top of this wildly exciting summer experience.

I felt like a character in a book as I lay stretched out across the top of the structure, tree limbs casting shadows across my face, hands folded behind my head.

One day as I lay in the sunshine, a helicopter flew overhead and dropped what appeared to be a roll of toilet paper from the sky. And then another. And another.

My Uncle Wayne was one of my favorite uncles. He and my Aunt Grace, whose hair he braided every morning, had a gaggle of children. My favorite, their youngest, went by Jaybird. Unlike Toboy, I never questioned the origin of the name; I assumed he went through a phase where he preferred to go without clothing. We are both redheads, his more strawberry than mine, and he always treated me like a little sister. Like the time we were on the top of a mountain and he explained to me in full theatrics that he had discovered bear tracks, and it would only be a matter of time until the bears found our location and ate us alive. As dirty tears streamed down my face, he said we should make a run for it. As we frantically burst through the screen door of my Aunt Grace's house, he doubled over in laughter. I had fallen for it. I always strove to impress my West Virginia cousins, and Jaybird was always there to encourage me. My eight-year-old brother had a speech impediment that summer and rolled his *r*'s, so all our cousins called him "city slicker," completely disregarding that the only city he had ever resided in was Nashville, not Boston, as the long *r*'s might have indicated. Brennan hated it. I hated it for him. We both knew being anything "city" was the biggest of insults. We were a family with a history of moonshining and cockfighting. Being "city" was the next worst thing to "the Law." But my accent was twangy and became twangier by the minute in the holler. When Jaybird told me I walked like someone who knew how to climb mountains, I took that as the greatest of compliments. To this day I approach every inclined rocky path with a sense of pride.

I loved these people who only saw me once a year but cared for me like their own. I could come and go in their homes as I pleased, except after dark, when my grandmother would have to call my aunt to come outside and watch me walk between the two houses out of fear I would be mauled to death by her numerous aggressive dogs.

Sneaking up on someone was historically a very dangerous situation in Harts Creek, West Virginia. You had to be invited. And that's why I knew at the sight of the first helicopter: *I do NOT think these people were invited.*

I remember that day like it was yesterday. I quickly climbed down that knotted rope and ran to the mouth of the holler to see if my cousin Brandy, my main sidekick that summer, had seen the toilet paper falling from the sky. (Sidenote: Brandy was always in love with my brother Brennan, both eight years old that summer, and she spent a good deal of emotional effort trying to convince him that fourth cousins do not count as relatives. As much as he wanted to shed his city persona, that was not the subject he cared to take the leap with.) About halfway down the holler, the dirt road turned to asphalt. As soon as my feet hit that asphalt, I saw it: a Humvee. It was the coolest thing I had seen all summer and I stared in awe, frozen directly in its path of travel. Uniformed men popped hands out to wave or more likely to say, "Get the heck out of the way, you clueless child." But I was soon joined by a band of other relatives, no one relaying an ounce of fear or concern as Brandy's mom, who I had not seen step off the couch all summer, joined the group with a full-sized 1980s camcorder fixed firmly on her shoulder. Evidently no matter what went down, she had plans to make money by selling footage to an afternoon talk show. We were all eventually ushered to the side of the road as a half dozen Humvees proceeded past us, all of us smiling and waving as if at a Veterans Day parade. I decided the best place for me was back to the treehouse. And so I ran, dust from the military vehicle tires on that old dirt road coating my hair and face. Up the rope and into the hatch, I sat in that newly constructed space to observe the rest of the day silently from cracks between tattered boards.

As it turned out, the white toilet paper–looking material falling from the sky was not toilet paper at all. They were markers dropped to identify certain areas of crops—specifically, illegally grown crops. My Uncle Wayne, who braided my aunt's hair in the morning and brought me freshly cut rhubarb in the evenings, my favorite snack at the time, had also been growing miles and miles of marijuana in that holler, which apparently had been detected by color from a helicopter in the sky. This was an actual, real-life FBI raid. My uncle and his older sons were handcuffed and arrested. My brother and I thought that it was hilarious when the FBI searched my grandmother's house. She never drank, never gossiped, and her only vices were coffee, cigarettes, and *Days of Our Lives.* But there they were with full authority, tearing apart her pristine sofa cushions, which until that point were flawless as they lived daily covered in flat bedsheets.

The FBI set that crop on fire in a hollow between two mountains. To this day I will always be the first to detect the scent of burning pot. The world around me was literally going up in smoke and I lay in the treehouse with a smile on my face, staring up at the sky, dreaming of my next construction project. Yes, I knew the circumstances around me were bad. My uncle was in big trouble. My aunt's life was about to change forever. But I was not afraid. I was wonderfully distracted. I had the treehouse, my first of many wonderful distractions that have allowed me to pretend that I have some control over the circumstances of my life.

As I grew older, I learned that there is no designing your way around the hardships of life. Decades later, our beautiful treehouse hung in shambles as the ragtag group that made the dream into a reality began to struggle with depression and substance abuse, one by one, including my little brother Brennan. Thousands of miles away, I watched from behind a computer screen in Boston, wishing I could transport us all back to that summer when we were eight and nine years old, scavenging, laughing, dreaming. We were happy. Distractions from the outside world were distant thoughts as we reveled in a world we built with our own hands, a world we controlled. Yes, it was the summer my uncle went to prison. But what stands brighter in my mind is that was the summer we built the treehouse, the summer I fell in love with design. So much more than fabrics and paint and fluff, we created something out of nothing. And that was the high I will continue to chase for the rest of my life.

THE WRITER'S
COTTAGE

The Writer's Cottage was the second project I designed for the Millers. Intended to be used as an escape from the real world, in many ways it reminded me of our West Virginia treehouse. When the project began, Don and Betsy were weeks away from delivering their daughter, Emmaline. With the trust I had gained through the Carriage House project and then the impending arrival of their first child, I was pretty much given creative liberty on the cottage. Preston Shea drew the plans and exterior elevation. Then it was back to me, with the help of Nathan, to dream up something big on the interior. Storytelling is Don's profession, and storytelling through interiors was very quickly becoming a part of mine. The Carriage House was not a historic building, but with the interior we told a story that would imply otherwise. At the cottage, we decided to do the same. We dreamed up a story of an original 1800s log cabin that was later updated and added on to. Nathan and I took a trip to Kingston Springs, a town thirty minutes west of Nashville. There, at a mill called Pioneer Lumber, we sat with the owner to select the wall material as well as the hand-hewn beams for the ceiling. I learned that the grout-looking material between log-cabin boards is calling chinking; I had Nathan test a half dozen different colorways of chinking until we felt like we got it just right. I found vintage glass-front cabinets and oversized industrial pendants, and I used both to create a more deconstructed kitchen of sorts, like back when people used to have all of their appliances freestanding in their kitchen.

Preston had drawn a typical gas-insert fireplace in the family room. As I studied the plan and referenced photos of more historic architecture, I came up with the idea to leave the niche, but instead of an insert, I'd use a freestanding cast-iron stove. I added the little window to really seal the deal on the charm factor. The dining area sits between the kitchen and family room and is visible along the very clear centerline that runs front to back through the middle of the home. I purchased the table from a local antique shop called Patina and Co., and the antique barrister chairs from a dealer in High Point. I loved the idea of using barrister chairs, also known as juror chairs, in a guesthouse. I know from experience, there is nothing more uncomfortable than seeing a broad-shouldered, large-statured man trying to enjoy dinner on a delicate antique chair. Juror chairs, on the other hand, were literally built to hold everyone (whether they liked it or not!). This set was vintage, with some wonderful signs of age, so all boxes were checked.

We very much designed this house back to front. So as if walking backward from the original log-cabin structure to the "newer" addition, we designed the long hallway to serve both corridor and coat-closet functions. And to keep the visuals clean, we used jib (or hidden) doors to enter the powder bath and laundry. The entry is the preamble—as you stand there, you can pretty much see in all directions of the home, including the sleeping porch, the log cabin, and the entries to each guest suite. But what you are most affronted with are the books! So many books. This is a Writer's Cottage after all.

With noted authors, musicians, and celebrities being no stranger to Goose Hill, I loved imagining who may stay in this cottage one day. For the guest suite on the right—the green, the floral, the proper-southern-lady wholesomeness of it all—I envisioned Laura Bush. And on the left, Michelle Obama, who wore a ton of purple while First Lady and gives total queen vibes, in my book. And canopy beds are for royalty, obviously. I read in Jenna Bush Hager's *Sisters First* (coauthored with Barbara Pierce Bush) that Laura and Michelle are indeed dear friends, and if they wanted to have a little writing retreat together, I believe I know just the spot.

My favorite story about this cottage is actually the one you are reading here. While photographing the project for my own portfolio, I received an email from my friend Kathryn with the subject line "Introducing you to my fabulous book editor." That editor, Juree Sondker with Gibbs Smith, is now my editor. What began with a book on an airplane written by storyteller Donald Miller will conclude with a book of my very own, telling stories the best way I know how—through interior design.

LEFT: I bought the pendant lights and the cupboards on a sourcing trip and knew in my heart that the Millers would approve without me bugging them for approval. Lucky for me and my bank account, I was correct.

ABOVE: The skirted cabinet was a perfect solution for a guest house that has very little storage needs.

ABOVE: I learn something new on every project. On this project: "chinking" and how to go about selecting a chinking color.

RIGHT: In every corner, a spot for reading.

What is a southern screen porch without a porch swing and loads of wicker furniture? We love this durable, easy-to-clean line by Summer Classics.

LEFT: We tried everywhere we could to implement thoughtful, well-detailed interior architectural elements.

ABOVE: Books, books, and more books. My clients as a whole are a pretty literate group.

We designed the sinks to sit perfectly on top of the chests we found from our friends at Patina and Co. And then the little antique mirrors, always. If you see me start to use store-bought, just tell me it's time to retire.

I designed this room for Laura Bush. To my knowledge, Laura Bush has never stayed here.

I designed this room for Michelle Obama. To my knowledge, Michelle Obama has never stayed here.

It really fills my cup to think of two intelligent, accomplished women who live in the public eye seeing past their political differences to become dear friends. I think we could all take a cue from that. And I am not exaggerating when I say that is the deeper motivation behind the story of these two spaces. The differences of each highlight the beauty of the other. What a sad story it would be if these two rooms were carbon copies of one another.

ABOVE: Each suite is designed with an attached bed nook perfect for children or extra roomies.

RIGHT: A place for writing in The Writer's Cottage, of course.

LEFT: This laundry room also holds brooms, vacuums, and a pull-down door to the attic—all hidden behind a jib door.

ABOVE: This base is an antique school desk I found at an antique event called "The Nashville Show." I still remember driving home with it in my trunk, high on my find. I do not do drugs, I do antiques.

CHAPTER 4

CONFESSIONS AND CONFESSIONALS

When looking back, design school was such a weird experience. I did not get into the program my first year of college. When I finally did gain admittance (after submitting an art portfolio during my freshman year at the University of Tennessee), I wanted it so much more than the average student coming straight out of high school. I was in a sorority, which I found to be a very positive and encouraging experience. They frowned on overdrinking and smoking cigarettes. We were required to make good grades, we had "big sisters" who showered us with gifts, and we were never short on a costume party to attend. To this day, I live for a costume party. My husband, on the other hand, pledged a fraternity. The first time I ever saw him, he was being paddled on the stage of a bar called Campus Pub while cupping his balls for dear life, literally. Fraternities are so weird. But design school might be even weirder.

During my first year we drew lines by hand, using very expensive pens we had to fill with ink ourselves. We did this a lot. We were later promoted to cutting foam core that we would then use to build models. But first it was just cutting—lots and lots of cutting. We were graded on the accuracy of our lines and the sharpness of our cuts, both shockingly harder than one would imagine. Run out of sharp X-Acto blades at 10 p.m. when the supply store was closed and it was pretty much over for you. Dull blades cut foam core like nibbles from a hungry mouse. My friend Dustin once cut off the tip of his finger during the foam-core era. Nine a.m. on a Tuesday he stood up in our studio of twelve and said in a monotone proclamation, completely lacking expression, "I cut my finger off," then he turned to the trash can, threw up, and proceeded to walk himself over to the student medical center. Our two-hundred-year-old professor (a former colleague of famed architect Ludwig Mies van der Rohe) just shrugged his shoulders like "Meh, that happens," and the rest of us all turned back to our drafting boards to continue cutting. Sorry, Dustin.

Second semester of that same year, under a different professor, we were assigned to design and build a confessional booth, as in what Catholics use to bear their souls (or so I have heard). I really loved the concept of the assignment, but the leap from tiny foam-core models to constructing a three-dimensional, occupiable structure was huge. We first-year architecture and design students rarely slept that semester, and with that level of delirium, we became pretty close. There was one-finger-down Dustin, who at that point I called Dusty; a Polish girl named Monica, with skin as translucent as mine and who shared my lifelong disappointment in not being born the correct race to allow us to identify as strong Black women (the most powerful of powerful women in our book); Jenny, a campus Young Life leader waiting for marriage to both drink alcohol and have sex; and a girl named Mandy, who was dead set on trying out for Playboy's "Girls of the SEC" that spring. We were young and tired and just learning how to be adults while simultaneously learning how to cut wood. We spent more time that year hovering over our gray drafting boards in a concrete building that had not been dusted since it was constructed in 1965 than we did anywhere else on campus.

The confessional-booth project nearly did us all in. My dearest friend in the class, Jenny, decided to make hers out of acrylic. Her concept was based on transparencies, and our professor loved it. But Jenny, after pricing the cost of custom-cut acrylic, regretted it deeply. Other than architectural school supplies, our biggest splurge that year was going to Jimmy John's on Thursdays for lunch. Design school professors do not really encourage you to think about things like how much money is in your bank account when presenting your conceptual ideas. As a recipient of financial aid, I kept my concept simple. Jenny, on the other hand, who probably had eight more dollars to her name at the time, is probably still paying off hers. My design involved a series of suspended, overlapping wooden picture frames with various metal mesh panels inside. A budget-conscious take on perceived privacy. It may have been less expensive but it was ambitious. At eighteen and nineteen years old, most of us had never even used a screwdriver. And we already had Dusty with his cautionary half finger glaring at us twenty-four seven. So, we nervously toiled late into the night for months until the day of the critique.

The morning of the critique was a trainwreck. I'm typically a fanatic about being on time, but somehow I'd overslept. And it didn't stop there. After basically living in the architecture building all semester, I woke up to discover I had no clean underwear. In a complete panic, I decided to go without. I wore light-khaki polyester slacks probably from Bebe (note: it was very on trend in those days to dress like a sexy banker) with no underwear. Did you hear me say light khaki? A two-hundred-pound confessional booth is not an easy thing to slide quietly into a critique with while running late. As I attempted to discreetly enter the room, which was not a room at all but a concrete balcony cantilevering over the center of the building, I was flustered trying to recall the presentation I'd prepared on the intersection of faith and architecture. And yes, again, I was wearing no underwear. The glare from my professor when I turned the corner affirmed my worst fears: she hated me. I was a deplorable human being who could not even stay on top of her inventory of clean underwear, much less make it to her final presentation on time. I was raised Baptist, not Catholic, with no real-life experience with confessionals or the Catholic faith. But from what I understand, both religions tee you up for a long life of crippling, self-induced shame. Just look at me sideways and I will confess something random I did twenty years ago. Case in point: this chapter. But by the grace of God—who, to my shock, did not strike me dead for going sans underwear in public—I somehow made it through the presentation and the semester, and after four years, I graduated from the University of Tennessee's School of Architecture and Design.

Close to a decade later, I became an adjunct instructor at the Boston Architectural College. I had dreamed of teaching at the college level, and I thought I was going to be so much better than my own two-hundred-year-old professors, who were honestly probably not much older than I am now. The students were going to LOVE me. They would hate me at first, of course, but then they'd adore me, like Michelle Pfeiffer in *Dangerous Minds*. At the winter break of that first year, I received my students' anonymous reviews of my performance as their instructor, all written in their own handwriting, which I had been grading for a full semester—so we'll call it anonymous-ish. A student I really liked, who I pushed because I knew she could be a great designer, wrote, "I am scared of her. I don't even like it when she comes to my desk. I am so scared of her." And as I sat in my little brownstone with that stack of papers, reading one after the other, all pretty critical, I thought I was going to fall over dead from laughing. Was I that oblivious? Had I at the ripe old age of twenty-nine become our two-hundred-year-old professor!? Surely not. No one had bled out in our classroom, and I didn't notice anyone having to forgo undergarments. But the next semester, three different students asked me to be their thesis advisor. And that, although way less glorious than it had been in my imagination, was my actual "Michelle Pfeiffer in *Dangerous Minds*" moment. They liked me. They really, really liked me. At least three of them did anyway. But who's counting?

Princeton Ave. came to me during the middle of COVID. The client had just fired their first contractor, hired their second, and was beginning the litigation process to recoup some of their lost funds. It was a wonky start to what turned out to be a great project. But what being a student and an adjunct instructor in design school had taught me was the process does not have to be shiny. Sometimes people lose a finger, sometimes people don't like you. It's never about being the most popular. It's about getting the best work possible out of everyone on the team, especially yourself. Because when that is the common goal, and the project is complete, you always forget the rest. Minus maybe the tip of your finger, but who really needs that anyway!?

PRINCETON AVENUE

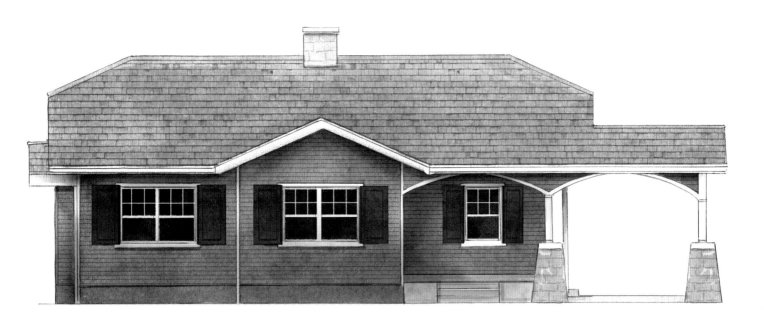

Our Princeton Avenue project, much like design school, involved some weird experiences. The first and foremost being the COVID pandemic. I had never met Eric and Eileen Evans prior to the March 2020 lockdown. After hiring me that following July, it would be almost eighteen months of working together before we would ever even fully see one another's faces. The home is in Richland Park, a historic neighborhood of Nashville. It is filled with modest-sized, character-filled homes. Sidewalks line the streets, and every Halloween they host a huge neighborhood-wide pumpkin-carving contest. The gut-renovation and addition of their 1930s bungalow was designed by local architect Michael Ward. Both young attorneys and somewhat newly married, the Evans were a delight to work with from the beginning. By Nashville standards, the home is not huge, so using every square inch was very important. There is no foyer, so when you walk in, you are immediately in the middle of the formal living room. Eileen envisioned this a space to host book-club meetings. We landed on a vibrant yellow green for the walls and a textured golden velvet for the sectional. The entire room wraps tightly around the original fireplace. No stranger to book clubs, I cannot imagine a better spot to host. Eric's office is through the adjacent French doors, and I love the abutting mix of feminine and masculine spaces. The primary suite was carved out on the first floor across from a guest suite designed with Eric's mother's personal style. We kept the newer, open area of the home fairly neutral. Eileen has a penchant for ovals, and with that in mind I found the antique dining table at one of my favorite dusty haunts south of Nashville. We had it stripped down to the original wood. Then it was on to figuring out the coffee table. Maybe she ran into a lot of sharp inside corners in her life? I don't think I ever clarified, but we landed on a custom oval plaster table for the family room, and I love the way the two shapes, in very different materials, play off of each other.

The Evans love their animals and at last count were the parents of two cats, Olive and Hazel, and a rambunctious golden retriever named Waffles. The animals were considered in most conversations, including the design of the upholstered window bench in the formal living room (the perfect cat perch), and in depth on the design of the laundry room, where there is a built-in litter-box cabinet as well as a cat door that allows them to go and hang out on the screen porch whenever they choose. The cats were cats and pretty much hated us from the start, proving it by scratching out the bottom of a brand-new upholstered ottoman shortly after install. But not Waffles. Waffles was our best friend and constant companion, whether we liked it or not.

The Evans hosted many of their young friends for long weekends and wanted the second floor to have a bed-and-breakfast vibe. We chose different wall coverings and trim colors for each space to really ring in the individuality, imagining guests saying, "I call the purple room!" The den at the top of the stairs will hopefully one day be a playroom, and each bedroom will become home to a greatly adored child. As we concluded our work on this project, Eric's mother unexpectedly passed away from breast cancer. Having lost my own mother a year before while still working on this project, and then seeing this sweet couple experience something similar, has really helped me realize that we can plan and decorate and dream but life is unpredictable. Good interior design does not insulate us from the inevitable pain that comes with being alive. It is an honor to design homes that will see both laughter and tears, homes for blowing out candles and bandaging wounds. It is a privilege as an interior designer to play a tiny part in creating the backdrops to the memories of lives well lived. And it was an absolute privilege to design Princeton Ave.

ABOVE: The charming scale of this original fireplace is something you rarely find in new construction homes. When the contractor suggested striping off the ornate details, and I looked at the client over the brim of my COVID mask with a look that said "It's him or me."

RIGHT: The custom-framed intaglios mounted on hand-made marbleized paper are sourced from our Nashville-based retail shop, Heirloom Artifacts.

FOLLOWING SPREAD: The fanciest cat bench in all of Nashville. Seriously, try and sit down, they will audible say in a Forrest Gump–accent, "Seat taken." Ask Jessica from my office—these are not normal cats.

I explain our approach to design and color like going from a hot bath to a cold pool. You do not appreciate one without the other. This example of moving from the saturated green to the airy neutrals is a good example of that concept.

FOLLOWING SPREAD: Our client had a penchant for ovals, as seen with the selection of this coffee table as well as the dining table pictured above.

LEFT: Sister Parish's Burmese used on the bed is a favorite of ours for scale and versatility.

ABOVE: We love using polyester velvet for high-use upholstery pieces. After raising four toddlers with a pair of chairs in the same fabric, it's a material I can personally vouch for.

ABOVE: Our client's antique cuckoo clock.

RIGHT: Again, with the antique mirrors. Can't stop, won't stop.

ABOVE: I found this antique sconce from an online antique dealer in France.

RIGHT: Another guest room that feels like a hug. Most of my colleagues had sworn off all shades of purple when I designed this room, still recovering from the obsession with Monica's apartment in Friends. So, this space looks sweet, but it's also kind of rebellious.

LEFT: This sweet guest bath was designed for our client's late mother, and I will always think of her and how much thoughtful care they put into creating a space that she would love.

ABOVE: Another room to clue us in on who the real boss of the house is. The cats.

CHAPTER 5

THOUGHTS ON BUNGEE JUMPING

I walked down to the city courthouse in Boston, Massachusetts, in May of 2010 to obtain a business license, officially hanging out my shingle as Sabbe Interior Design. Less than a year later, I gave birth to my first child, Remi. Truth be told, I'd thought I would be a stay-at-home mom. I'd spent years in commercial architecture firms, working late nights under insane deadlines, and I knew that was not compatible with the type of motherhood I aspired to. But continuing to build my months-old business when Remi was born was exciting. I could not imagine saying no to either. So, I kept doing what I had been doing since I was fifteen—working. Except now I was working with a child and zero childcare. My husband was in his second year of medical residency, and we were living on borrowed money in an incredibly expensive city. The extra income I was able to provide working while also raising a baby gave me a sense of pride and accomplishment I had yet to experience at that point in life. I remember typing emails at my desktop computer while simultaneously breastfeeding my baby halfway strapped into his Bjorn and thinking, "Nope, there is nothing I cannot do." My husband worked what felt like all the time, so often it was just Remi and me, blazing this new trail together. I took him to vendor meetings and on job sites. I don't know if it was being in New England or my newfound confidence as a business owner, but I made no apologies for traipsing through every facet of the profession with motherhood hanging all over me. Coming from a very stiff corporate background, it felt a little wild, and I loved it. I was once wrapping up a meeting with two male contractors, gently rocking my baby in his car seat at my feet, only to realize he had totally slept through his feeding and I was wearing the evidence in two large circles on my shirt. I slid on my jacket and smiled, "Guess that comes with the territory." I weirdly enjoyed making them uncomfortable, having been made uncomfortable so many times in the male-dominated architecture firms where I'd spent my twenties. I was making my own rules, running my own firm. Even if the firm was just me, my baby, and my leaky boobs.

I had our second son, Wells, in 2013. We then moved back to Nashville and had our daughter Georgie in 2015. After a lot of prodding, persuading, and maybe a couple of alcoholic beverages, I became pregnant a fourth time. Thank you, Bryan Sabbe. One major blessing in my life is how easily I become pregnant. A second major blessing was not being sexually active in high school because I would have for sure been a teen mom. But by my fourth pregnancy, I was thirty-five years old and my ob-gyn called my pregnancy "geriatric." "How dare they?" I lamented with a group of girlfriends shortly after finding out the news.

"You should totally take the fetal DNA test!" they told me. "You can find out the gender early. And it's free because you are thirty-five." Always eager to start dreaming up my next interiors project, in conjunction with the zero-dollar cost, I was sold. The following week I asked my ob-gyn for the test. The test was supposed to be extremely accurate at detecting all sorts of fetal abnormalities, none of which I cared about; I just wanted to know if I could do scalloped curtains in the nursery. I went to my appointment; they drew blood and sent me home. A week later my ob-gyn called and said, "Is Bryan home?" I said yes. She said, "I am sorry to tell you that your baby has Down syndrome." I asked if there was any chance that the test could be inaccurate. She said, "I'm sorry, this test is 99.6 percent accurate. Make plans." Before I hung up, I asked if I could know the gender. "A girl," she said. Another girl, how perfect. A sister for Georgie. And then I sat on the floor and cried.

Interviewing for projects as a pregnant woman and the sole owner of a design firm had always felt like a slight disadvantage. Interviewing for projects as a pregnant woman who had shared on social media that her unborn child was going to have special needs was downright painful. I felt sharing it honestly was the right thing to do. I really had no clue what my life was about to look like and I wanted potential clients to make choices based on what felt right to them. Then one day the Garrisons called. They were a young family who had just purchased one of my

very favorite homes a block from our own house. A house that I once contemplated sticking a note in the mailbox to see if they would share the exterior paint color with me (Horseradish by PPG). Both husband and wife are successful attorneys. Lucky for me the Garrisons didn't bat an eye at my bulging belly and unknown future, so we began phase one of what would end up being a six-year project from start to finish.

We started with the formal living room, dining room, and sunroom. The home's layout was similar to my own, and I found the process to be very natural. They liked what I liked, and each presentation was met with resounding excitement. I designed all three spaces while I navigated my future as a special-needs mom. We reached out to a local childcare facility called First Steps. My dear friend Jane threw a baby shower where instead of gifts, everyone donated to our local Gigi's Playhouse, a Down syndrome achievement center. I even drew plans for a garage apartment behind our house where our daughter could one day live. I bought a fetal heartbeat monitor, and every evening I lay in the corner of our breakfast nook behind the table to listen to her little heartbeat. And every day I designed the Garrison residence. As I specified furniture and fabrics, I dreamed of my daughter who would one day work with me in my studio. She would be funny and kind and have a head full of red hair like me. To rebel she might get a job at the local grocery store, but I would woo her back to the design firm with cool music and free decor. We were well past the mourning phase and on to planning. She was our girl, and we were going to be better people because of her. I read all the books, had lunch with other special-needs moms, and even named her Cora—a name that had never been on my list but seemed easy to say for someone who may not speak well until she was five or six. I attended a dinner party the night before she was born. My friends made a cake that read, "Happy Birthday, Cora," and I told them that I felt like I was about to bungee jump for the first time. I was excited and had been for months and months. But now it was go-time, and I was terrified.

I went into labor the next morning. Everything was as routine as it had been with my other pregnancies but, as a favor to my husband, who is a pediatric anesthesiologist, a neonatologist was in the room when she was born. Before I pushed, I announced defiantly, "This baby has Down syndrome. Do not feel sorry for me. I do not feel sorry for myself." Everyone assured me that they had already read my chart and did not plan to take pity on me, my least favorite sentiment. I pushed twice and out she came, screaming at the cruelty of the cold room. Something was not right. The books said she would be weak and floppy. I held her for a second, said hello, and looked at her palms. The books said she would have a crease down the middle of her hand. There was no crease. The neonatologist took her to the examination area where I heard him say, "This baby does not have Down syndrome." Bryan came over to my bedside and repeated, "They do not think she has Down syndrome." Annoyed, sad, and frustrated, I replied, "Can you please hand me my baby?"

She was born on a Friday, and we would not know her official diagnosis until the following Tuesday, as labs closed for the weekend. And so I sat for two days and stared at this little stranger, wondering. As I gained a little more gumption, I started holding her up to ask the nurses, "What do you think? Does this baby have Down syndrome?" It made them all incredibly uncomfortable. And the hilarity of the discomfort made me laugh. "Just take a guess, I won't hold you to it." In my mind and heart I had become pregnant, lost that baby, became a mother to a very real baby with special needs, and then lost her too. Now I was holding this third, new baby. She was beautiful and awesome and bore the second baby's name. But I didn't know her at all. And I missed that other baby. I will always miss that other baby. The one who would have reminded us daily of strength in weakness. The one who would have always made us smile when we thought back to how scared we were when we first realized who she was and how silly it seemed now. The one who would most likely live with us forever.

A friend and mother of a daughter with Down syndrome was the first to call me when I gave birth to Cora. I remember her saying, "Yeah, she's cool, but you're kicked out of the club for sure." I laughed. If you know me, you know I had planned to lead all the parades, host all the playdates, and here I was, kicked out of the club entirely on day one. So many people prayed for us during that pregnancy, and I tell the story of Cora's birth often but not to tell a story of God healing my baby, because I do not think people with Down syndrome are broken. It's a story of God healing me. I like to plan my future, and I like to know the outcome. I work in a field where we plan for months, sometimes years, to create predictable outcomes. But with Cora I needed to walk to the edge of the platform, with no assurance of the outcome, and I needed to jump. I landed in a completely different spot than I'd planned for, and I landed with a completely different heart as well. The pediatrician called the following Tuesday to confirm: "Your baby does not have Down syndrome."

I installed phase one of the Garrisons' home three months after Cora's birth and the final phase the week before she started kindergarten. The story goes that the man who lived in the home before the Garrisons had been in one of the September 11th towers and survived. He and his wife moved to Nashville, bought the house, and she channeled her grief into decorating. Years later, I did the same. Design is always good for that, giving us a sense of control in an otherwise chaotic world.

This past spring when Cora walked across the stage for her preschool graduation, the director announced, "Cora Leigh Sabbe wants to be an interior designer just like her mother when she grows up." As she stood there, teeny-tiny in front of a huge crowd, smiling and waving to us, I could not help but think back to the days of me lying in the corner of our breakfast room listening to her heartbeat and wondering with fear and excitement how this story would turn out. Drapery is hung and Cora is well. One chapter ends and another begins.

BABY

FEET

BOWLING AVENUE

David and Erica Garrison are both highly accomplished attorneys, and I am not sure if it was their love of the law or the photos I spotted of them with former presidents on their bookshelves, but the interior style of their home is very much what I would classify as classic American—a concept brought home with our liberal use of red, white, and blue. Red is not a color we get a lot of requests for, and ultimately I blame our mothers and the '90s, but I am a strong believer that no color should be fully eliminated from the palette. Originally built in 1920, the Garrisons' home had been decorated by the previous owner in the early 2000s in a style that is often referred to as "transitional," but again I'll blame the '90s. Our goal was to bring her back to her original glory, to stop making the architecture do all the heavy lifting and let the interiors have their moment.

The dining and formal living spaces were designed in the first phase and very much serve as balancing weights on opposite sides of a scale as you enter the home. We used complementing shades of blue and varying scales of pattern to achieve this, with the goal being to create visual symmetry while avoiding contrived matchy-ness. Two years after phase one, the Garrisons hired local architect Van Pond to draw an addition to the home that would include a primary suite, great room, and new kitchen. The family of five hosts everything from holiday gatherings to political fundraisers, and the additional square footage allowed this historic home to meet their modern needs. After living in Boston for five years, that city's Public Library Reading Room is one of my forever inspirations with its enormous vaulted ceiling and intricately detailed arched windows. Many elements of the Garrisons' great room derive from that space, specifically the built-in bookcases and use of heavy architectural moldings. Similar to the Boston Public Library, the reading room feels like a completely unique space. We chose to do the same with the great room, painting it a saturated green and furnishing it with warm woods, smart stripes, and woolen plaids.

The kitchen and primary suite were designed as a reprieve from the grandeur of the great room, both hinting back to elements of the original architecture with their subdued palettes and overall restraint. We came up with the concept of using two complementary wallpapers to help bridge the transition from new to old. For the original home we chose the Veronique pattern by Les Indiennes, which greets you at the entrance and carries you through the second floor as well as to the backside addition. Then, where the original home meets the addition, we transition to Golden Lily by Morris & Co. I find that the best historic architecture celebrates additions and changes over time by intentionally expressing transition from new to old. With that thought in mind, I try to do the same with the interior of historic homes.

After almost five years of working together, designing the three children's rooms on the second floor was our third and final phase. As if we had been hired by three individual clients, we worked with each child to express their own personality and preferences. From Minecraft and outer space to baseball and ballet we strived to design sophisticated spaces that checked all the childhood boxes while also allowing each box to be unchecked when interests one day inevitably change. And after six years I have decided that children's rooms, which are filled with pure joy and anticipation of who that child will one day be, should most definitely always be the grand finale of a project that spans over half a decade.

LEFT: I first spotted this wallpaper pattern in the hallway of my friend Jane Abercrombie's house at her annual Christmas party. It was love at first sight. I used it in a different colorway but I'm sorry I copied you, Jane. Please still invite me to the Christmas party.

ABOVE: This framed arch is original to the home and one of the many types of historic details I like to take inspiration from for our new construction projects.

There is nothing I love more than a back-to-back sofa situation. I am not often a matchy-matchy designer, but the ideational mirroring of both sofa and pillows in this instance felt like it honored the original formality of the space.

These clients actually owns their own books. Lots and lots of real books read by real people, such a rare treat as a designer in this era of the handheld device.

ABOVE: My clients saw this chandelier on their honeymoon years before we designed this space and knew it was exactly the right piece for this space.

RIGHT: I love the visual layering this central butler's pantry provides.

ABOVE: More is more for us when it comes to mixing patterns. Also, I want to be buried in a casket with horizontally lined fabric.

ABOVE: This corner just screams "Make happy memories here!"

RIGHT: And this corner screams "Grab a blanket, let's take a nap!" Houses need both in equal parts.

FOLLOWING SPREAD: This room was inspired by the Boston Public Library. I love how the painting by Kayce Hughes gives it a focal point while stealing zero attention from the interior architecture.

ABOVE: My clients brought these ladder-back chairs from their previous home, and we lucked out by finding the perfect antique trestle table to pair them with.

RIGHT: Some spaces are an exhale, but not this one. This one is an inhale of the cleanest, freshest breath you'll take all day.

LEFT: Three shams and a bolster: that is our absolute max when it comes to decorative pillows on a bed. And this coverlet by Taylor Linens is hands down our most frequently used bedding item.

ABOVE: Proof that the practice of restraint is not beyond me.

ABOVE: We loved using red in this home just because no one was really using red right then and it felt rebellious. Rebellion is one of my main motivations in life.

RIGHT: First Lucy liked pandas and then maybe dolphins. Luckily her parents took a bit to get around to letting me design her room. By then Lucy had agreed, her likes would change overtime; let's avoid a theme at all cost.

ABOVE: He loves space and camping. Not to brag but I think we nailed it. But no, it's not a theme.

RIGHT: Again with the red. This bathroom gives me *Home Alone* vibes. Who doesn't get warm fuzzies when recalling the *Home Alone* house?

CHAPTER 6

GEORGIE!?

People constantly ask me, "How do you do it!?" They are most often referring to my kids and my job, maybe staying married to my husband. Just kidding, Bryan Sabbe—if you ever leave, I'm coming with you. I know it's meant to be a compliment, but I was raised by a single mother with very limited resources, so I always want to reply, "Are you kidding!? This is easy." I have a husband and a reliable car. And food! Sometimes if we're feeling wild, we'll even shop at Whole Foods. For me, going to the grocery store without having to add up how much we are throwing into the cart feels like a luxury. It's a luxury my children will never understand, and it honestly makes me sad for them because a genuine appreciation of this luxury has been such an unexpected gift in my adulthood. I can try to explain it, tell them stories of cutting coupons out of the Sunday paper with my mom. But until you take something off the counter and put it back because you can't afford it, you'll never grasp the delight that is my experience of a trip to the grocery store. I draw the line at the economy-size tub of cheese balls they attempt to smuggle into our cart on almost every trip. I cannot let them skim through childhood without some form of trauma. I kid. I feel sure they will have plenty of stories for their future therapists, like the thirty seconds in the fall of 2017 when "How does she do it?" came frighteningly close to "What has she done?"

I was just beginning to feel like myself again after giving birth to our youngest, Cora, two months prior. It was that sweet season of life where we were not yet shuffling four little people from one sports practice to the other—another hectic season I'll for sure miss one day. It was hectic then too, but we spent long, lazy afternoons visiting, my favorite activity, while our young kids rode tricycles and bounced on trampolines. One afternoon, my kids and I were at the home of my dear friend Jane, a born hostess. Her house was a popular afternoon spot in those days,

149

where moms looking to bridge the afterschool-to-bedtime hours were always coming and going. Years later, when someone asks me how I know someone, I often say, "We met at Jane's, back when the kids were babies." All roads led to Jane, and we are all indebted to her approximately ten thousand dollars in Costco snacks to prove it. Jane, like me, loved to visit. When it was time to go, she'd say, "Grab some goldfish, kids! We need to finish this story," then we'd pick back up with our conversation knowing none of our kids were going to eat a proper dinner that night—but who cared?

That day at Jane's there were four moms and their kids, then three moms . . . and then just Jane and me and my crew, still going strong as the afternoon turned to evening. I finally yelled for my crew, "We're leaving in five!" As I made my way toward my shiny new minivan, with tiny Cora strapped in her car-seat carrier hanging from the crook of my arm, the boys followed, jumping in the far back, and Georgie sat next to Cora in her car seat in the middle row. All but Cora had mastered the art of buckling and unbuckling at this point, so I was feeling uncharacteristically confident. "I am totally killing this four-kid thing," I thought. Then Wells, five at the time, yelled, "I left my shoes under the trampoline." Refusing to let pass my moment of parental pride, I responded, "Stay in your seats, everyone! I'll be right back." I pressed the button for the back door to slide shut, then jogged up the hill to the

trampoline. I grabbed Wells's shoes, ran back to the van, jumped in, and threw the shoes on the passenger seat. On the two-block ride home, my boys sang at the top of their lungs, "Lord, I Lift Your Name on High" along with the radio. Pause here and understand, I played Cardi B during those years in the car too—clean versions, but nonetheless, those tiny ears were familiar with "WAP." But that day we were holy rollin'. As my babies sang sweetly, I truly felt like I did have it all together. Was four kids a lot? Sure, but I could handle it. I was equipped for hard things. I was ready to print an achievement award to pin to the kitchen corkboard alongside the children's art and months-old birthday-party invites when I pulled into our drive and glimpsed Georgie's empty seat. "Where is Georgie!" I screamed to my boys, who casually replied, "She got out." To which I screamed, "Why did no one tell me!?" Evidently, while I'd been grabbing Wells's shoes, my three-year-old daughter, wearing her princess dress and a stack of bracelets halfway up her little arm, unbuckled and got out of our van, closing the door behind her. Neither of my four- or six-year-old children had thought it at all concerning that their three-year-old sister was wandering the streets of Green Hills completely unsupervised, as they sang praise-and-worship music at the top of their lungs.

I ran into our house and screamed for Bryan to watch the three who'd made it home, jumped into our other car, and sped back to Jane's. On my way I called to tell her the situation and heard her husband call out, "Georgie! Georgie! Honey, where are you!?" with sheer terror in his voice. It occurred to me briefly that Keith would never let me babysit his kids after this. To this day that remains true. In the two minutes it took to get back to their house, they'd found Georgie in their backyard playing with their dog, Kip. I raced over and reached down to pull her into a hug, filled with relief. "Georgie, honey," I pleaded, "why did you get out of the car!? You scared me!" She said simply, "I wanted to play with Kip." As I buckled her in and drove us home, my hands shaking, my brain conjured the millions of other dangerous things my kids could do without giving a second thought. She'd just wanted to pet a dog.

I rocked two-month-old Cora to sleep that night, crying softly. "I had no business having another baby," I thought. "I can barely manage the three we already had." But when I shared the story with a few trusted friends, they each had a story to share back about how their mom/aunt/grandma/neighbor once did the same. "It's big-family stuff," they assured me. "It happens."

Though that recollection will always make my stomach flip, it gave me perspective. Chaos is part of life. I get now how tragedies happen. When I think of the parents who have accidentally left a sleeping baby in the car, of the toddler who wandered briefly out of sight only to be found in a swimming pool, my heart aches. In an instant, the question goes from "How do you do it?" to "How could you let that happen?" I ache with those parents. This thing called parenting is crazy. If we fully understood how crazy, most of us would be too scared to attempt it in the first place. I speculate it's why our bodies are the most fertile when we are young and dumb.

How do I do it? My house is a mess. When I designed it, I fantasized about how my children would line up on the four stools eating fresh-baked cookies just out of the oven. In reality, they eat frozen corn as an afterschool snack—their idea, not mine—and I could not care less. Who has the time? I am literally doing my best to not run any of them over. I neurotically count heads now, and to make my anxiety even more debilitating, we've added two cats and a dog to the chaos. My minivan, no longer new and shiny, is so messy that our carpool buddy recently volunteered to take some trash into his house to discard for me. We're falling apart at the seams over here, just like everyone else. But when I lie in bed at night, no matter if my house and van are trashed and my kids have declared I am the worst mom ever, I know how lucky I am. And it's not the circumstances of my life—the food, the husband, the functioning car—that make me feel lucky. It's the awareness, the understanding that through the highs and lows I will always have the honor of being their mama. And for me, that is the greatest gift of all.

EATON COURT

When I met Katy and Bucky High, they too were raising four kids. But unlike me, they were doing it in thirteen hundred square feet . . . while homeschooling. And to my knowledge, they had never forgotten any of those children in a friend's driveway. Homeschoolers win the "How do you do it all?" competition in my book. But Katy, a former schoolteacher, and Bucky, a tax auditor, were indeed doing it all inside an adorable Cape Cod–style home on Eaton Court, minutes from downtown historic Franklin, Tennessee. Yet on our first site visit, as adorable as it was on the exterior, I was struck by how inefficient the interior of the home was for such a large family. Believe it or not, thirteen hundred square feet is plenty of space, if you spend it wisely. I spent years living with babies in Boston on a resident's salary and my second child slept in a closet. It can be done. But to be done well, it must be strategic.

In the High family's case, the primary bedroom was consuming close to a quarter of their home. So, for this family of six plus a dog and a squirrel—yes, Brad the squirrel, the apple of his human mama's eye—I put on my best space-planning hat, dusted off the skill sets I learned in my corporate interiors days, and came up with the most efficient home I have ever created. Aside from a tiny bump-out for the primary bath and office, we created a whole new home—all under the existing roof.

As you enter the home, you are greeted with a subtle but impactful pattern called Marigold by Morris & Co. We used it in the entry, up the stairs, and throughout the children's landing. It helped set the tone of "our house is traditional, but we are a young, fun, energetic family who lives in every square inch." To the left, we maintained the original living room; on the right, we converted the original den into the new primary suite—both painted in saturated hues of green and blue and both centered around original fireplaces. The just-over-two-hundred-square-feet addition off the primary bedroom allowed for a bathroom, closet (with laundry), and small home office. We omitted the barely used formal dining room and combined that function and square footage into the now larger kitchen. It's important when creating efficient floor plans to make sure they are not so efficient that there is no longer room for the extras of life—the bustling of extra bodies during the holidays, a playing toddler on the floor, or in this particular instance, a giant German Shepard always lounging nearby. I like a kitchen with room to breathe. And with the added windows and new French door spilling out onto the back patio, this new space has plenty of room to breathe.

With the parents relocated downstairs, the upstairs became the children's domain. We divided the formerly huge primary suite into a shared bedroom, children's den, and double-vanity bathroom. We maintained two of the existing bedrooms and carved the original outdated bath into both a full bath and laundry closet. The sofa in the children's den pulls out into a bed. The efficiency of this entire home takes me back to the days of designing in cities like New York and Boston. Sometimes we are just decorating, filling huge space with more and more until it no longer feels like huge space. Not the case with this project. Every piece of art, every bit of furniture, every bit of everything was carefully considered with the mindset of more is more . . . but not too much. In this home, too much would have absolutely been too much.

LEFT: This front entry connects via the stairs to the children's landing. With that in mind, we chose a wallpaper that would work in both spaces.

ABOVE: And it was all yellow! We like an energetic mudroom. As if the walls were yelling, "Hurry up, grab your shoes, get out the door!"

ABOVE: To squeeze more function out of this somewhat compact home, we eliminated the formal dining room and chose to capture that function down the center of the kitchen, which created a truly lovely "heart of the home."

RIGHT: I had a previous client tell me that if you wanted your child to come home and tell you about their life, you had to provide a cozy spot in a space with lots of activity for them to chat with you without having to sit eye to eye. With that in mind, I try to incorporate a single cozy chair in both primary bathrooms and kitchens when possible.

LEFT: We came up with a cost-effective idea of having the children's silhouettes made by an artist on Etsy and then having our local framer add wider mats to really give interest to the overall visual of this fireplace area.

ABOVE: This sweet chair was another find from our dear friends at Patina and Co.

This room is a love story. The husband secretly purchased radiant heat flooring for his wife, who tends to feel cold much of the time.

Everyone deserves a little privacy. That's how we design our bathrooms. No one needs to see another person floss their teeth. Ever.

LEFT: This room, with the original fireplace, was formerly the family room. It now feels like the coziest little bed and breakfast.

RIGHT: We, as a design firm, are in a pencil-post-bed era and we're not ashamed to use one on every single project.

ABOVE: Two teens of different genders share this little bath. May God bless them and keep them, may his face shine upon them and give them peace. Amen.

RIGHT: Jenny Lind beds forever.

This sofa by Lee Industries in the children's den is a sleeper. Pick up the Barbies and, violà, guest room.

LEFT: The little ladies who reside in this bedroom also share a bath. Luckily they both like pink.

ABOVE: Back-to-back vanities, one for each girl, maximize the floor plan and allow a plethora of storage for all of the Drunk Elephant products they most definitely will not need for another twenty years.

CHAPTER 7

CHARLES EAMES
WAS A CHEATER

I met Bryan when we were in college at the University of Tennessee, Knoxville. I was nineteen and he was twenty. I had seen him around campus and thought he was completely '90s rom-com–level cute, a fact that he still pretends to find insulting to this day. I, on the other hand, always the funny friend, assure him that I would be thrilled to be deemed someone's trophy wife.

It was sophomore year and my boyfriend at the time had picked me up from the Architecture Building, where I was working away since earlier that morning. He gave me a once-over and declared that I needed to go up to my dorm and make myself "look more presentable" for the fraternity bonfire. It was much like that moment in *Legally Blonde* (which I could recite word for word back in 2001) where Elle Woods says, "I'm sorry? I just hallucinated." I asked him to pull over, dramatically yelled "We. Are. Over." and slammed the door of his pickup truck. I believe his response was, "You gotta be effing kidding

me." I marched up to my dorm room and flipped through the Greek directory until my finger landed on "Sabbe." I called Bryan and left a message on his answering machine with a wild disregard for who other than him might press play: "Hi, this is Stephanie Frye. Some of my friends are going with some of your friends to my sorority's formal tomorrow and I wondered if you want to go with me." He called back and said yes. Five years later—and a lot of chasing him around local bars in feather-trimmed tube tops while he acted uninterested—we were married. As I've shared, rejection only fuels my fire—future father of my children included.

Bryan graduated UT with a civil engineering degree. I dreamed of us being the next Charles and Ray Eames: cute, married, artsy, famous. Charles Eames was one of the most influential American architects of his time, his most widely celebrated creation being the Eames lounge chair. He married Ray, who had a background in painting, and the two embarked on a life of creativity together. Twenty-year-old me thought, "Where do I sign?" Years later, I watched *Eames: The Architect and the Painter*. Spoiler: Charles Eames was a cheater—a sort of Don Draper of architecture. I was gutted, but once recovered, I thought, "Bullet dodged." Always the planner, I plotted a life for Bryan and me that would be drama-free. We'd be happy, work hard, make good choices, and live a quiet life free of chaos. Oh, sweet Stephanie, if you only knew.

We were married at Vine Street Christian Church in Nashville on a warm June day. Like my mother and that tiny Free Will Baptist church, I chose it for the architecture. My younger brother Brennan walked me down the aisle. Bryan and I lived in Memphis the first three years of marriage. In our freshly married days, I worked at a local architecture firm and Bryan attended medical school. We bought a small yellow bungalow directly across the street from a dilapidated triplex that reminded me every day of the beige-vinyl-siding condo scandal of my childhood. But Memphis was a beautiful city. There were sidewalks and so many architecturally intact historic neighborhoods. There were also startlingly high crime rates and heartbreaking poverty statistics, but we were young and naive and thought our generation would be able to fix it all. I tutored on the weekends at a local high school where I helped soon-to-be graduates write their first professional résumés, emphasizing the importance of creating new email addresses that absolutely could not include the phrases "sexymama" or "babygirl." It was the best part of my week, and those girls taught me so much more than I taught them. Some evenings after work I rode my bike down to nearby Cooper Young to browse the used bookstore or peek in the window at the cat shop, being a bona fide cat lady way before Taylor Swift made it cool. I recall thinking, "This is exactly what I thought adulthood would look like." Then one day Brennan called. After a bit of chit-chat, he said, "Hey, two things. First, Allen (our dad) is in the hospital having a quadruple bypass and I think you should come into town. I think he might die. Second, we have another brother. His name is Jason."

It's funny to me how you can grow up and try to make good choices and live an honest life, but you will always be your parents' child. My parents' choices, good and bad, will always be a part of me. I learned that day that my dad had a girlfriend before he met my mom and she became pregnant while they were together. When she let him know she was expecting a child, he said it was not his and never spoke to her again. Three years later, he met my mother. Two years after that, I was born. All while my brother was being raised by his single mother fifteen minutes away from our house. It was twenty-six years before I knew that brother even existed.

As this information flooded through me that day in Memphis I thought, "This was absolutely not what I thought adulthood would look like." This was in fact an episode of Jerry Springer. I called my mother, who did not seem shocked, replying only, "If he [my dad] told you I knew, I didn't. He only mentioned it once when he was drinking, so I didn't believe him, and he never brought it up again." Basically, she knew. If it were possible for heads to implode like characters in cartoons, mine would have been in pieces that day. Here I was, two years a Sabbe, having married into the least drama-filled family I knew, an adult by all standards but still swimming in generational chaos. Yet something came over me almost immediately that said, "Your parents' drama does not have to be yours."

So, I called the older brother I never knew I had, and we made plans to meet at Pancake Pantry in Nashville. Jason told me when his mom passed away the year prior, he had decided to go on a journey to find his biological father. He found him. Our dad never denied the story as Jason knew it and assured him that his life had most definitely been better off without him as a father—a sentiment our dad had shared with me on multiple occasions too. We laughed at how easily he let himself off the hook since, in fact, both of our childhoods had been quite hard. Yet Jason grew up thinking our dad had chosen another family, one in which he had found joy and purpose. That he was fifteen minutes down the street parenting other children, coaching their baseball games and attending their dance recitals—that is the part of this story that will always break my heart. My most vivid childhood memory of my father was him coming home so intoxicated that he punched his hand through a glass window as my mom screamed, and how the police arrived shortly thereafter. Brennan was too young to remember, and Jason was decades from being in our lives. They both grew up with a dad-sized hole in their hearts, yearning for something that I knew to be fiction. My hole started to scab over that day the police came. If that's what dads were, I was fine not having one.

On a Saturday morning, at twenty-six years old in a booth at Pancake Pantry, I became a proud little sister and have worn that title with joy every day since. We got a late start, but we have already lived so much of life together. Jason and his family moved to Nashville a couple of years ago to be closer to us. He and my husband have become like brothers, and my children have never known life without their favorite uncle living fifteen minutes away from his little sister once more. Sadly, two short years after we all met, we lost our baby brother Brennan to suicide. Seven years after that, our dad died alone in a parking lot from a massive heart attack. My mom died five years after that from breast cancer. I look back with so much fondness on the person I was in my early twenties—the one who thought she could plan her life, make good choices, and somehow escape the chaos she was born into. She was sweet, and sometimes I am jealous of her ignorance of what was to come. But on the flip side, she hadn't met her wonderful older brother Jason, the sibling who would see her through her thirties, forties, and God-willing, decades more. She was not yet the mother of the most amazing four humans she has ever known: Remi, Wells, Georgie, and Cora. She didn't yet know she'd own her own firm where she would be paid to tell people all the design minutiae that had ruled her thoughts since childhood. She couldn't have dreamed she'd be celebrating eighteen years of marriage to the boy across campus, whose family hilariously turned out not to be as drama-free as she once thought, and who will always and forever be '90s rom-com–level cute.

WHITLAND AVENUE

During my first meeting with Whitney Fuller, I had the same "This is going to be a good one" feeling as I did when I first met my husband. She opened her three-ring binder to show me inspiration for her project and I realized, "Wait! That's my work!" I was familiar with seeing images from more accomplished designers' portfolios during those initial meetings, and this was the first time anyone had shown me my own and it felt like a really big deal.

Whitland Avenue is a highly coveted street within a highly coveted historic neighborhood of Nashville. There are sidewalks and Fourth of July parades and a historic overlay that has left the charming architecture of better days almost entirely intact. The Fullers' home was originally built in 1930 as a duplex, converted at some point over the years very awkwardly into a single-family home, and then reconfigured again by Rachel Martin with local architecture firm Pfeffer Torode. Rachel and I went to design school together, and it was such a treat to get to partner with her on this project.

Upon entry you are greeted with a photograph by Jack Spencer. To the left is the formal living room, and to the right is the library. The furniture arrangement in the formal living room draws you into the space with its ongoing layers. The chaise allows the room to not be broken by an unfriendly backside of a sofa. I love rooms with multiple functions, and the little corner game table is a great example. We chose various scales of pattern and were intentional with avoiding anything too matchy. The goal of our work is to imply it has evolved over time.

The view from the formal living room through the elevator vestibule and breakfast nook to the back wall of the kitchen is one that designer dreams are made of. So rarely do we get to see so many materials and patterns stacked so neatly from one vantage point. The breakfast room itself layers pattern on top of pattern on top of even more pattern. If there were a central heart of this house, the breakfast room is it. All other functions spin off this central space, so we chose to give it as much bang for the buck as possible.

The kitchen overlooks the backyard, and the afternoon shadows cast from the old-growth trees beyond give it an almost treehouse feeling. We chose a neutral sage for the walls and one sofa to really allow the windows to be the star of this space. As you look inside the scullery, the refrigerator is located to the right. A lot of people would have pushed back on separating this piece from the main kitchen, but in terms of convenience, it allowed the kitchen to feel less utilitarian and more like an extension of the keeping room. The scullery is also where we hid all small appliances, placed a second sink plus dishwasher, and still had room to carve out a desk for Whitney. It, too, is a happy little space with large windows and low-level lighting. I chose to tile the walls floor to ceiling after taking a trip to the Biltmore during the design phase, always being drawn aesthetically more to service spaces over more formal, proper hosting areas in historic homes. (Think *Downton Abbey*!)

The keeping room may be one of the coziest rooms we have ever designed. We collaged several pieces of the Fullers' existing art over the English roll-arm sofa, upholstered in the perfect Penny Morrison stripe. The slipper chairs on the ends can be turned to face the kitchen or stay toward the fire. The Carolina Irving–clad armchair is the cherry on top of it all.

Because this house embraces our "more is more" mantra, we wanted to give a reprieve to all the pattern in the primary suite. We will often have several more restrained spaces in our work to allow an emotional response to the contrast. To use one of my favorite analogies, it is going from a hot tub to a cold pool. For the busy mother of two, this room is an escape. The bathroom with floor-to-ceiling beadboard and freestanding clawfoot tub feels very spa like.

The second floor is home to the two daughters' bedrooms as well as their hang out–homework loft. We wrapped some of the same color and pattern styles into the area but added a layer of cheerfulness that says, "This is space is for us."

LEFT: Game tables are such a fun forgotten piece in most modern-day homes. We use them often. Who doesn't love a game of checkers while you wait on your carpool ride!?

ABOVE: We love using a chaise or tête-à-tête to elongate rooms so that no one is walking into the backside of a piece of furniture.

ABOVE: I took a trip to London for my fortieth birthday during the design phase of this project and these little sconces by Soane were one of my favorite finds.

RIGHT: The home is historic but the wall paneling, we designed that. Adding this level of interior architecture to our projects is one of our favorite things.

LEFT: My client actually collects first edition, autographed books. This is not styling. This is real life.

ABOVE: The Fullers' existing console paired nicely with the painted round table by Tritter Feefer.

ABOVE: Another example of more being more.

RIGHT: The name of the game with this home was visual layering. So often how we see it on a design board is not how it translates into a final space. This home is the exception.

LEFT: We hid the refrigerator in this kitchen just beyond that pocket door in the scullery. No farther away than if it were a completely open kitchen but required a slight mindset shift that the Fullers have reported to have zero regrets about.

ABOVE: This kitchen is on a third story and feels like a treehouse as you gaze out into the backyard.

FOLLOWING SPREAD: I have never loved a collection of textiles in one space more than I love this one.

We used the primary suite as a palate cleanser, an escape from the pattern and the color and maybe the children too.

Something old, something new, something blue.

I sourced the pendant from Etsy and that's where we started. This is hands down the happiest windowless room we have ever designed.

Teen lounge dreams.

CHAPTER 8

ALMOST HEAVEN

We began renovating the exterior of our home in Nashville shortly after our youngest daughter, Cora, was born. I'm a tortoise when designing for myself. I take my time, and nothing ever feels quite finished. Plus, I have been at this profession for almost twenty years—at this point, when I'm not working for other people, I really just want to be a mama and a wife. I want to lie in bed and read books and drink coffee. I've been to therapy. To paraphrase Taylor Swift, the old [trauma-decorating] Stephanie is dead. So, we'll get there when we get there. But several years ago, the work on our exterior garnered some attention from passersby, as we live on a busy street. A lady once knocked on my front door to ask me for details on the paint color. On another occasion, a letter arrived in the mail that read "I used to live in your house in 1930. If you would like to meet, please email me." It was like the opening scene of a Nicholas Sparks novel. I immediately called my next-door neighbor, Cathy, a mahjong fanatic who winters in Naples and reminds me of Ouiser from *Steel Magnolias*. When we renovated her house a few years ago, she actually made one of my employees cry. After I ignored her for a week, she finally apologized. But I love her like a second mother and consider her a very dear friend all the same. Cathy has lived in her house since the 1980s, and when I told her about the email, she said, "Impossible. I know of everyone who has lived in your house. That man is lying." When I asked why someone would lie about spending their childhood in my house, she replied simply, "People are weird." Again, envision Ouiser.

I do not disagree, people are weird, but I decided to email him anyway. He was able to describe the layout of my home exactly, right down to the post at the bottom of the steps where he said his father hung his hat and coat after work. So, I decided he was definitely not a creep and invited him and his sister over for a tour. A couple of weeks later, they arrived on my front porch. As we walked through the house, they told me stories of their childhood—roller skating and annual holiday parties. Like my husband, their father was a physician. They had another sister who had already passed away who slept in the room my boys now share. The other sister slept in the room that my girls currently share. The teeny, tiny room that we used for Cora's nursery was where the youngest in his family—the man who wrote me the letter—had slept as a child. To really bring the Nicholas Sparks–vibes home, I asked him to hold Cora for a photo, which he kindly agreed to. It made my heart so happy when they said I had excellent taste and had done their childhood home justice. As we descended the stairs into our basement, the brother-and-sister pair became quiet. With tears in her eyes, the sister looked toward an elevated room that I always thought was built to keep things dry in our otherwise damp basement. She said, "That is where our nanny slept." She continued, "Our father would come down and set out Coke crates when there was water down here so she could get out without getting her shoes wet. "My God," I thought, "this house has seen some sad stuff."

When we initially bought the house, I asked if the previous owners had died in the home. I knew them to be very elderly and the idea of someone having died there really creeped me out. I was assured that no one ever had. Eight years and two more babies later, we moved my mother into what was our playroom. She had terminal cancer. And just like when I was young, my brain went into full-fledged design mode as a coping mechanism. I found an antique full bed and a gray Pottery Barn sofa on Facebook Marketplace. I ordered a rug my dog had yet to destroy with her pee from my local carpet rep. "Hillary," I sobbed, "my dying mother is moving in with us and I am about to have a thousand-pound hospital bed delivered. The rug needs to get here before the bed. I cannot let her spend her last months on a rug with pee stains." We mounted a TV on a retractable arm facing her hospice-supplied bed. I hung art around the room and made sure all the lamps had 2700-watt bulbs, then braced myself for the actual hard part: waiting for death.

My mom and I were not close before she came to live with us. Things had been done and said that had led to basically no relationship at all. But my brother Brennan was gone, and my mom was basically alone. She'd lost a lot of relationships as she struggled with her mental health over the years. We'd had lots of conversations and therapy sessions about boundaries and what healthy relationships looked like. We never got anywhere with all of that. Now I was helping her bathe and brush her teeth. I hired Val, an amazing nurse, who stayed with my mom while I worked and until I arrived after picking up the kids from school.

Bryan and I had told my mom that Val was hired by hospice so that she would not feel like a financial burden, then one day I came home to Val laughing in my kitchen. My mom, loosened up on pain meds, had told her to watch out for me, that I was a "rich bitch who only hung out with people in Belle Meade." This was the part of town where my retail shop, Heirloom Artifacts, and design studio are located. The spaces resides in a 1960s strip mall across from a pay-by-the-hour daycare and an out-of-business Krystal fast-food restaurant. My mom, and her cherished melamine plate, always had me figured out.

I had a mental list of things I believed I could never do before she moved in and I eventually did everything on that list. It's amazing what we can do when there is no one else to do it. Scared, sad, uncomfortable or not, I was standing on the edge, bungee jumping again.

Though I had help, the mental load was crushing at times. At a construction meeting in the early stages of a project on Parmer Avenue, I got a call from Val. I answered and heard yelling in the background. My mom's breast cancer had metastasized into her brain at this point (a good pass, I decide, for the "rich bitch" comment, although hilariously in character regardless). She'd become convinced Val was trying to kill her. She insisted I come home and save her. Nothing I could say would convince her otherwise. I left the meeting and silently cried in the driveway with the phone still pressed to my ear, mouthing, "I'm fine. Everything's under control." I lied. But what was I supposed to say? That my dying mother had run into the traffic on Woodmont Boulevard because her nurse, who felt like my only friend, was trying to kill her?

My mom wrote a note to me before she lost her ability to write. She said in so many words that she was sorry for not being so great of a mother to my brother and me at times. I wrote back to say, "I forgive you." Neither of us ever mentioned it. We mostly sat alone watching *Matlock*, except for the times my four- and 6-year-old daughters came in to host fashion shows or perform dance routines. I made a playlist of songs I remembered my mom playing when we were kids, including John Denver's "Take Me Home, Country Roads." When she lost all ability to communicate, we listened together as he sang, "Almost heaven, West Virginia," and I whispered in her ear that she would be able to see her baby boy again very soon.

We had our first and last mother-daughter slumber party in that room the night before she died: June 9, 2022. My mother was the first to die inside our home in its one-hundred-year existence. I have lived here just shy of ten years and under this roof I have rocked my babies, kissed my husband, and ushered my mother into heaven. Though a home may look pristine from the exterior, a life well lived rarely is. And when I consider that I designed a room for my mom to die in that was her literal almost-heaven, I realize dying in a home is just as natural and beautiful as living in it.

"We need to find a way to tell when the cat's around and when she isn't," said another.

Many plans were discussed and rejected. Finally, one mouse announced what he thought to be the perfect solution.

"The problem with the cat is that she's so quiet," said the mouse. "What if we tie a small bell around her neck so that every time she moves, the bell will tinkle? That way we'll always know where she is, and she'll

38

never be able to surprise us."

"Brilliant!" said one mouse.

"Perfect!" said another.

"What a wonderful plan!" exclaimed a third.

Everyone agreed that putting a bell on the cat was the solution they were looking for. When they were finished congratulating one another, the oldest mouse spoke up:

"Putting a bell on the cat sounds like a good idea, but tell me, which one of us will do the job?"

39

Stephanie

you h...
...accept my apolog...
I love you so very much,
Mom

PARMER AVENUE

The Parmer Avenue project came to us during a very hectic season. We were the busiest we had ever been in the office, and then a couple of months into the project, my mom moved in. Billed as a renovation, the entire home minus the slab and the garage were the only parts saved from demolition. The team on Parmer was probably the most-experienced, construction-involved team I had ever been on. Erin Cypress with Pfeffer Torode was the architect. Erin is kindhearted, detail-oriented, and really helped me sharpen my eye for interior architecture during the span of this project. She introduced me to new interior door styles, casings, crown-molding assemblies. Erin explained how she didn't love plinth blocks and taught me how to detail backbands. It really was the most educational experience I have had in a long time. The builder, Matt Daniel, has built some of the most phenomenal homes in Nashville; and the clients, Char and Hunter Ford, are two of the most laid-back, down-to-earth people I have ever worked for.

The preliminary design very much centered around the kitchen. We began by suggesting a shift in the layout of the appliances, centering the sink on the windows while allowing the island to be fixture-free. I spent time researching historic homes, and one common theme with the early American-style architecture that I love the most is huge cooking fireplaces. We obviously planned to use a gas range and not a cast-iron stove, but we designed a hearth-style surround and worked to detail the millwork to make it really feel as if it had been there for a hundred years or more. The blue-and-white delft tiles on the backsplash were selected to help emphasize this idea of a "new-old home." The evening room was my second deep dive into the design process. The room is tiny but packs a big punch in terms of function. We hid the TV behind bifolding doors above the fireplace. Hunter ties fly-fishing ties as a hobby—I think he actually sells them at a few local shops—and a small card table was selected with that function in mind. There is a walk-in closet next to the fireplace that houses an organized fishing-tie supply that would give Martha Stewart a run for her money. We wallpapered the ceiling in this space, which is an element we chose to repeat in the primary suite. We love designing colorful homes, but for continuity we try to find a tie that binds so that each room does not feel like walking into an all-new experience. This tie was a natural-color grass cloth. Another major tie that bound in this project was the trim color. Instead of going with a standard white, we decided to do a darker, nonwhite neutral throughout, only changing shades in the primary bedroom and evening rooms.

I love to scour antique shops and flea markets to find original pieces to make new homes feel one of a kind. For Parmer, more than half of the lighting was purchased as antiques and rewired just for this project. The vanity and fireplace mirrors are also all antique finds.

The primary bathroom is also one of those spaces that I feel like you need to walk through to fully understand its magic. The checkerboard floor, marble tops, and cabinets painted in the same general Khaki Shade by Sherwin Williams transport you to a time when tiny, intricate details carried way more weight than they do in the new construction world today. The little oval window Erin designed is the cherry on top.

The foyer was our last space to design. There was a beam that needed to run along the backside of the original structure to be able to support the new second floor. That beam created a jut-out into the stairwell that to me, if we were not careful, was going to read exactly like the 1990 spec-house ledges that people decorated with baby carriages and silk ferns. Erin and I spent a lot of time thinking over the detail and finally landed on sloping the ledge, so there was no ledge, then covering the entire space with a nondirectional wallpaper to basically blur all of the hard lines created by drywall edges. Of all the little details, my favorite of the entire project turned out to be the little bookcase under the stair. While sketching the ledge, I came across that little piece of dead space and thought, "Now aren't you just begging for a cute moment." And there it happened. All in all, I feel like the "architects of old"—the architects who created the actual historic homes of Nashville—would have been really proud of us on this one.

LEFT: Our client's antique chest was the perfect first-impression piece for this old-world-vibe entry.

ABOVE: We spent a great deal of time with the architect detailing the angled window ledge shown here at the top of the stair. While in deep contemplation, we also discovered dead space at the foot of the stair where we were able to interject a bit of old-home character with the built in bookcase.

LEFT: If you have ever smelled the scent of hickory wood burning in a true masonry fireplace, that is what this image smells like. Absolute heaven.

ABOVE: I went to a local lumber mill where I ran into a guy I went to high school with wearing a shirt that said "I like hot moms," and that is where I found the antique beam you see in this image. He recognized me from twenty years ago. Maybe I'm a hot mom after all.

The visual of the copper gutter intersected by the vintage beam—chef's kiss. I'll pretend I planned that.

I selected a hand-painted delft tile from England for this backsplash and everyone said, "Takes too long, Stephanie! Find something faster or pick something else." So I found this on Etsy. The vendor adds decals to Daltile tiles and refires them, and I honestly cannot tell the difference.

We really spent time on this project to find as much antique lighting as possible, including this sweet chandelier. I find no greater joy than replying "Sorry, it's vintage" to anyone who asks for sourcing via Instagram direct messages.

ABOVE: I never thought I would say it, but cabinets do not really have to go to the ceiling in all situations. I learned that from the Brits. Americans will say, "Dust ledge!" Your interior designer, who secretly worries she may have gone too far, will reply, "You don't even clean your own house!"

RIGHT: This powder bath is male. He wears a tweed tailored suit, the perfect musky cologne, and a gold wedding band. You can't have him, but he's still fun to look at.

LEFT: I love these brass Devol taps we used in this butler's pantry. Along with full-height cabinets, mixing valves are very overrated.

ABOVE: Per my client's request, I designed this fireplace to have a hidden television above the mantle. Turns out it is a small fireplace and the proportional TV is literally the size of Michael Scott's TV in the episode of *The Office* where he and Jan host a dinner party. I really wish I could open those doors and show you.

FOLLOWING SPREAD: It looks like a game table (it is), but what it is actually used for is tying fly-fishing flies, a hobby I had yet to learn about until being hired for this project.

When we design beds like this, I think in my head, "You're welcome, husband." Husbands really do not love needing instruction sheets on how to properly make their new beds.

Both of the furniture pieces here originally belonged to my client's grandmother. I love storytelling with furniture like this.

The fruits of our window-ledge-detailing labor in full effect. I kept telling everyone, "The ledge cannot be flat, it will look like those ledges where people put antique baby strollers and fake plants" They all knew what I meant. Cladding it all in wallpaper helped bring it all home.

A senior-level architect I worked under at my first job out of college used to say "No brag, just fact" all the time. This bathroom is one of the best feeling, truly historic-looking spaces we have ever designed. No brag, just fact.

LEFT: Another cozy guest room with a bed-and-breakfast vibe.

ABOVE: The mirror is vintage, and I had the cabinet maker stain the wooden knobs to match.

CHAPTER 9

A FOREVER WORK
IN PROGRESS

I suppose the upside to having all of the people who have known you the longest no longer alive is that you are pretty solid on the fact that everyone dies. In forty-two years, I have undoubtedly experienced my share of loss. After losing twenty-six years of knowing one brother, I lost the other to suicide. Three months later, there was a massive flood in Nashville and my childhood home was completely destroyed along with any remnants of my mother's sanity. Two months after that, she was diagnosed with breast cancer while living in a camper in the driveway of her uninsured, now destroyed home. Four years later, my dad died. Five years after that, my mom followed. My role in my little family of origin, albeit self-appointed and a bit delusional, was "The Fixer." From a very young age, I cleaned and organized. I decorated. I watered plants and I cut grass. I learned to sew. As far back as I can remember, I had big plans of bootstrapping our family out of depression and addiction, out of broken relationships and financial insecurity. We were going to be the Cosbys (this was before the fall of Bill), except white and far less educated. I gave the eulogy at my brother Brennan's funeral. He had joked with my dad a couple of weeks before his death about me being a neurotic planner. He said, "Stephanie plans every step of her life. I bet she has a date on a calendar of when she plans to get pregnant." And as I stood in front of a packed room filled with so many people who loved my brother so dearly, I shared that, yes, I had plans. But plans do not always pan out.

Interior design is a profession based on planning and dreaming. Our clients say, "Once I have a pantry, I will actually start cooking again" or "Once we have a bigger house, we will host." It is my job to sit and dream with people: *How will this floor plan flow on a holiday? What will be the first thing you see when you walk through your front door every evening?* We plan and plan and plan some more. But at the end of the day, what we are planning is just a series of rooms in a house, not a life. Sure, we can figure out a lot of things—where we charge the electronics or how we store the shoes. But a new bedroom will not save a failing marriage any more than a stunning nursery will ensure that the baby will grow up to become a happy adult. Interior design has been so incredible for me over the past twenty years, but one thing I know for fact—contentment is not found in a well-appointed home. As someone who has lived on both sides of the tracks, I can confirm that lasting joy does not reside in a specific area code. I grew up believing that if I could just live in the *Father of the Bride* house, I would live the *Father of the Bride* life. Decades later, I now know that brick and mortar and a rose-covered trellis are indeed beautiful parts that make up a house, but it's the people living inside that make a home.

Our home in Nashville will never be "finished." Other than the half dozen projects I have started and not completed, we have outdated can lights in no particular pattern spread throughout our family room, plaster that pops off of the walls of our almost-one-hundred-year home in more corners than I can count, and a dog who shares the family penchant for anxiety and expresses that by peeing on only my favorite rugs throughout the house when the world gets to be too much. *And girl, I get it.* I cannot even keep up with laundry, and just this morning washed a load of towels for the second time after opening the lid to an overwhelming waft of mildew. But my favorite memories of home, the ones that I will remember when I am old and gray (god-willing) reflecting on a well-lived life, will not be a scene you would see in a magazine or even the preceding pages of this book. My memories rarely recall wall color or drapery pattern. My favorite memories of home include fifteen mismatched chairs crammed together around a candlelit dining table meant for eight, tiny flour fingerprints along the breakfast-bench cushion with holiday sprinkles covering the floor. My favorite memories are little feet running down our staircase toward stockings hanging from the fireplace. And sure, the stair railing is wobbly and the fireplace leaks, but old-lady me will absolutely not remember those details. Or maybe she will, and she will yearn for the days when she heard herself constantly yelling, "Stop hanging on that handrail! It's going to fall off!" And most recently, I get so much joy lying in bed at night and listening to my children, who share bedrooms, talk to each other about life as they know it while they drifted off to sleep. A little piece of their childhood they would not have had we ever saved up enough money to build out our attic as we have always intended. Unrealized plans are not always a tragedy.

I recently shared with my husband that for the first time in my life I really have no big goals. The planner has no plans. I have spent my life thus far on a white water rapid, being tossed around and around, but now I am in a lake. Both figuratively and literally. We recently finished building a small cottage on a lake about two hours south of Nashville and as crazy as the waters that led me here were, I think I would not fully appreciate the stillness without them. When I sit floating, straddled atop pool noodles in the middle of the water, I look back and see the house I have spent so much time designing and it brings me so much joy that I was able to use what God has gifted me with, what I have known would be my profession since I was eight years old, to be able to create such a special place for these people that I love so dearly. Then the silence is broken as the screen door flips open, smacking the wall beyond, and I hear, "M-AAAAAAH-m!" and in that moment I know, although still a work in progress, what I am looking at is far better than a house. What I am looking at is home.

ABOVE: In a world of styled photos, this is not one. These are my people and that is their wife/mama. No matching pajamas; a Taylor Swift nightgown and my son probably slept in that Titans jersey. And guess what, I'm not even wearing a bra. You're welcome.

RIGHT: The sun coming up over the lake, casting shadows on the walls of this little kitchen, is one of my favorite mental snapshots I have saved it in my brain for life.

ABOVE: Joey, my dear photographer friend, woke up at the crack of dawn to capture these shots so I would not feel compelled to style them. Fact: I never wore that apron. As I mostly just heated up frozen pizzas, it seemed a little excessive.

RIGHT: It's a sectional, it's skirted, it's striped (in Perennials Taton Stripe), it's cleanable, and it folds out into a queen bed. It's the Swiss Army knife of seating and I am very proud.

LEFT: This house is 1,600 square feet without a single inch of wasted space, but I still included these moments of pause. The paintings are by my friend Laurel-Dawn Latshaw.

ABOVE: At one point this summer I found them putting ice in their swimsuit bottoms and then jumping into the lake to thaw out. I really wish I had a sister.

ABOVE: The medicine cabinets have outlets inside for charging toothbrushes and razors. I do not joke when I say zero wasted space.

RIGHT: This room has a vaulted ceiling and so the stripe reads like a tent.

LEFT: This is what bunk beds look like when you tell your children to make their beds. Pinterest lied to you. After the recent addition of the trundles, still hardware-less and unpainted, this room sleeps nine. And unless I make nine beds daily, which I do not plan to do, this photo about sums up what a bunkroom actually looks like.

ABOVE: Waiting on a pair of antique sconces to be rewired, but that was my view from my office this summer.

ABOVE: This is the view while sitting in a swivel chair by the window of the family room drinking a cup of coffee. We are at the end of a cove, which gives us an amazing sense of privacy that is rare in an otherwise dock-filled lake.

RIGHT: One won't keep his hair out of his eyes and the other would shave his head bald if I let him. In so many ways, they feel like two of my oldest, bestest friends.

ACKNOWLEDGMENTS

Biggest of thank-yous to Jessica Kreutzer and Joey Bradshaw for helping me give birth to this book. You two made the grueling job of photographing my work an absolute joy. (Ellie, you too!). And thank you to the rest of my office for keeping things running while we were out taking glamour shots.

Thank you to all my clients—you let me live out my childhood dream. Being trusted to create the place you call home is the greatest of honors.

Thank you to all the architects I have worked with to design these homes, especially Erin Cypress and Rachel Martin. Thank you also to all the builders and craftsmen who have made the construction process such a joy. Nathan Chadwick, you really need to come back to the dark side.

Thank you to Juree Sondker and everyone at Gibbs Smith. I would never have written a book had you not asked. Thank you to Ami McConnell for your editing help, and thank you to Tauseef Ahmed for your beautiful illustrations.

Finally, thank you to my husband, Bryan, whom I have yet to let read this book but who once asked me, "Are you sure you want to put it all out there?" (I mean, what else am I going to write about—paint colors?)

And thank you to my babies: Remi, Wells, Georgie, and Cora. Being a designer is fun and all, but being your mama is the absolute best thing I've ever been.

FLOOR PLANS

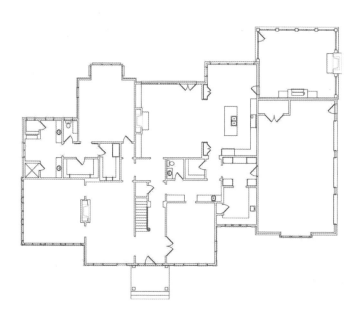

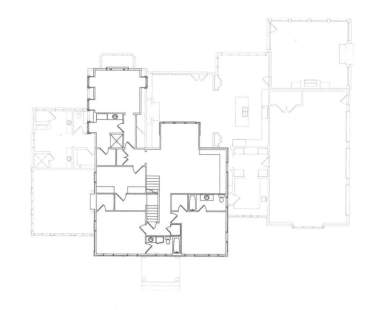

1st Floor

2nd Floor

LEIPERS FORK

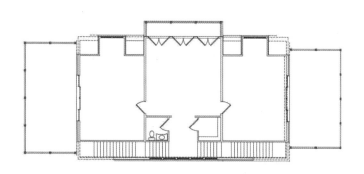

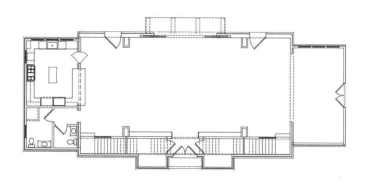

1st Floor

2nd Floor

THE CARRIAGE HOUSE

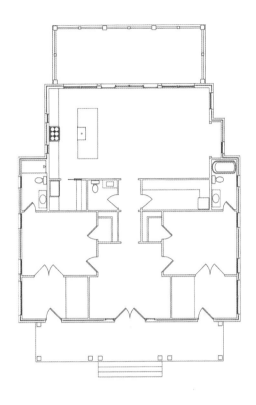

THE WRITER'S COTTAGE

1st Floor

2nd Floor

PRINCETON AVENUE

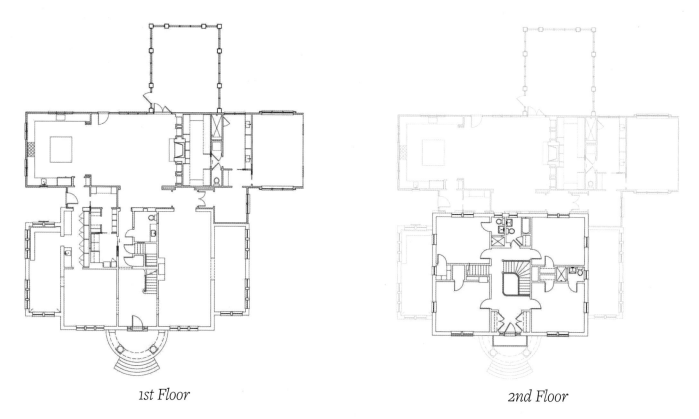

1st Floor   *2nd Floor*

BOWLING AVENUE

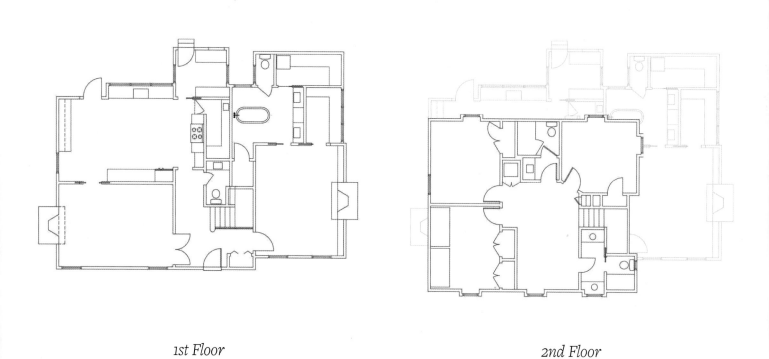

1st Floor   *2nd Floor*

EATON COURT

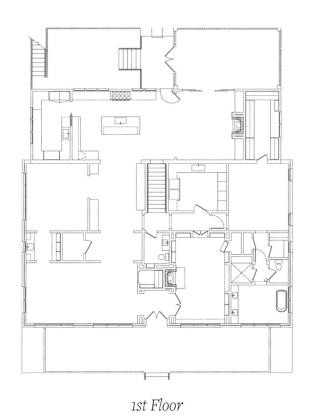

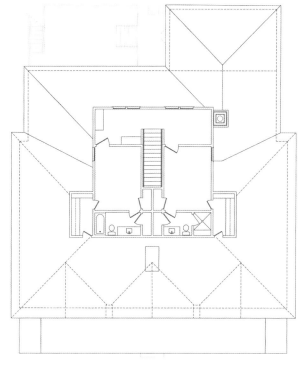

1st Floor   *2nd Floor*

WHITLAND AVENUE

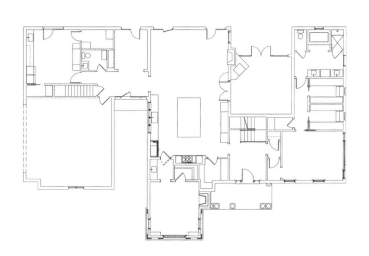

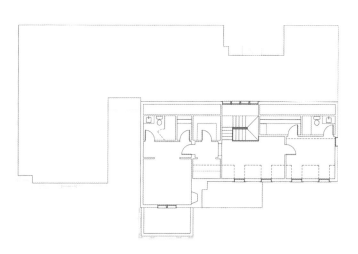

1st Floor   *2nd Floor*

PARMER AVENUE

MATERIALS

Endpaper Fabric
Olive Sacking in Cocoa by Guy
Goodfellow Collection

Chapter 1: Leipers Fork

Entry
Walls and Trim: Benjamin Moore,
BM-165 Water's Edge
Door: Benjamin Moore, HC-188
Essex Green

Living Room
Walls: Oscar De La Renta,
P2017100.540.0, Sameera Paper,
Sapphire/Gold
Trim: Sherwin Williams SW 7008
Alabaster White

Sunroom
Walls: Benjamin Moore, BM-473
Weekend Getaway
Trim: Benjamin Moore, HC-122 Great
Barrington Green

Kitchen and Breakfast Room
Walls: Scalamandre, WSB00441014,
Kersti, Spring Green
Cabinets and Trim: Benjamin Moore,
OC-45 Swiss Coffee

Dining Room
Walls: Kravet, BR-69504-845,
Zarafa, Sephia
Trim: Sherwin Williams SW 7008
Alabaster White

Family Room
Walls: Philip Jeffries, 3367, Grass Roots
Erics Ecru
Cabinets and Trim: Benjamin Moore,
HC-133 Yorktowne Green

Hallway
Walls: Sandberg, WSB 0036 0838,
Linnea, Misty Blue
Trim: Benjamin Moore, BM-165
Water's Edge

Primary Bath
Walls: Thibaut, T72854, Beverly Hills,
Mushroom
Trim: Sherwin Williams SW 7008
Alabaster White

Children's Bath
Cabinets: Benjamin Moore, HC-148
Jamestown Blue

Laundry Room and Guest Bath
Walls: Sherwin Williams SW 7008
Alabaster White
Cabinets and Trim: Benjamin Moore,
HC-112 Tate Olive

Primary Bedroom
Walls: Jasper, 5002-02, Devonshire,
Brown

Trim: Benjamin Moore, 2142-20
Turtle Green

Guest Bedroom
Walls: Robert Kime, Robur 0341B
Trim: Sherwin Williams SW 7008
Alabaster White

Children's Bedroom 1
Walls: Benjamin Moore, HC-150
Yarmouth Blue
Trim: Benjamin Moore, HC-148
Jamestown Blue
Ceiling: Sister Parish, SPW 2500,
Blue Orange

Children's Bedroom 2
Walls: Brunschwig & Fils, P8015145.13.0
Trim: Benjamin Moore, HC-126
Avon Green

Chapter 2: The Carriage House

Dining Room
Walls: Kravet, Simply Sisal-Haze,
#WNR1212
Trim: Benjamin Moore, HC-158
Newburg Green
Ceiling: Rose Tarlow, 4104W/03, Ming
Blue/Sea Mist

Gathering Room
Cabinets and Trim: Benjamin Moore,
HC-158 Newburg Green

Kitchen
Cabinets and Trim: Benjamin Moore,
496 Chopped Dill
Tile: Mercury Mosaics and Tile, Medium
Diamond Tile (Colors: Amber, Saddle
Tan and Starburst)

Loft
Walls and Ceiling: Morris & Co,
Melsetter Wallpaper, Apple Indigo
Antique, 216690
Trim: Benjamin Moore, HC-158
Newburg Green

Office
Cabinets, Trim, and Ceiling: Benjamin
Moore, 2145-30 Brookside Moss
Walls: Aesthetic, Edinburgh, Smoke,
EDI-45

Bathroom 1
Cabinet and Trim: Benjamin Moore,
BM-1197 Pumice Stone
Walls: Les Indiennes, #55 Veronique,
Chocolate

Bathroom 2
Cabinets: Benjamin Moore, 2145-30
Brookside Moss
Walls: Zak + Fox, Auspicious I Jang Koo,
ZFAUW-01

Chapter 3: The Writer's Cottage

Kitchen
Island: Benjamin Moore, 2145-60
Terrapin Breen
Ceiling: Benjamin Moore, OC-39
Timid White

Entry
Walls and Shelving: Benjamin Moore,
OC-39 Timid White

Guest Bath 1 and 2
Walls: Benjamin Moore, OC-39
Timid White

Guest Bedroom 1
Walls: Living Spaces, Sibylla
Trim and Ceiling: Benjamin Moore,
OC-39 Timid White

Guest Nook 1
Walls: Howe at 36 Bourne Street,
Thimble Prints, Cypress, Cocoa
Trim and Ceiling: Benjamin Moore,
OC-39 Timid White

Guest Bedroom 2
Walls: Lewis and Wood, Papyrus,
Desert Sand
Trim and Ceiling: Benjamin Moore,
OC-39 Timid White

Nook 2
Walls: Lake August, Sea Garden, Pacific
Trim: Benjamin Moore, OC-39
Timid White

Powder Bath
Walls: Benjamin Moore, OC-39
Timid White

Laundry
Walls and Cabinets: Benjamin Moore,
OC-39 Timid White

Chapter 4: Princeton Avenue

Formal Living Room
Walls, Trim, Mantel, and Cabinets:
Benjamin Moore, 2144-10 Guacamole

Kitchen
Cabinets and Trim: Benjamin Moore,
OC-24 Winds Breath
Walls: Benjamin Moore, OC-57
White Heron

Living Room
Cabinets, Mantel, Built-Ins, and Trim:
Benjamin Moore, OC-24 Winds Breath
Walls: Benjamin Moore, OC-57
White Heron

Master Bedroom
Walls: Phillip Jeffries, Bermuda

Hemp, Ecru
Trim: Benjamin Moore, HC-473
Weekend Getaway

Hallway
Walls: Morris and Co, Marigold, Linen
Trim: Benjamin Moore, OC-57
White Heron

Master Bathroom
Walls, Trim, and Cabinets: Benjamin
Moore, OC-57 White Heron

Guest Bath
Walls, Trim, and Cabinet: Benjamin
Moore, HC-149 Buxton Blue

Guest Bedroom
Walls: Carleton V, Marais, Leaf
Trim: Sherwin Williams Ruby
Violet 9076

Mother-in-law Bath
Walls: Schumacher, Versailles, Blue
Trim: Benjamin Moore, OC-57
White Heron

Laundry Room
Walls, Cabinets, and Trim: Benjamin
Moore, 2094-50 Desert Rose

Chapter 5: Bowling Avenue

Note: Porter Paint, when still in
business, carried a color called Umber
White. Porter is now PPG. PPG has the
formula and will still make Umber White
even though it is not a color in their
current line.

Entry
Walls: Les Indiennes, #55 Veronique,
Indigo
Trim and Door: Benjamin Moore, 169
Polaris Blue

Formal Living Room
Walls, Cabinets, and Trim: SW 9137
Niebla Azul, flat

Dining Room
Walls: Benjamin Moore, HC-83
Grant Beige
Trim: Benjamin 1649 Moore Polaris Blue

Butler's Pantry
Walls: Morris and Co Bellflowers,
Indigo/Linen
Trim: Sherwin Williams 9134 Delft Blue

Great Room
Ceiling: PPG White Umber
Beams: SW 7628 Windfresh White
Walls, Trim, and Cabinets: PPG Dark
Sage PPG1124-6

Hall
Walls: Morris and Co. Golden Lily, Indigo

Trim: PPG White Umber

Breakfast Room
Walls: Morris & Co, Honeycombe, DMOWHO106
Trim: PPG White Umber
TV Den Walls and Trim: selected and installed by previous owner

Kitchen
Walls: PPG White Umber
Cabinets and Trim: Sherwin Williams SW-9173 Shiitake

Primary Bedroom
Walls and Trim: Sherwin Williams 9137 Niebla Azul

Primary Bathroom
Walls: PPG White Umber
Trim, Doors, and Windows: Sherwin Williams 9137 Niebla Azul

Powder Bath
Walls: Jasper, JAMMU - Original, 5006-01
Trim and Cabinets: Sherwin Williams 7592 Crabby Apple

Children's Room 1
Walls: Strala, Peach, WP-STR-PEACH
Trim: Benjamin Moore, 2135-50 Soft Chinchilla

Children's Room 2
Walls: Philip Jeffries 2810 Moondance, Blue
Ceiling: Cole and Sons, Fornasetti, 114/28054.CS.0
Trim: Benjamin Moore, 518 Sterling Forest

Children's Bath
Walls: Sherwin Williams 7592 Crabby Apple
Trim: PPG White Umber

Chapter 6: Eaton Court

Foyer/ Stairway/ Playroom
Walls: Morris & Co, Marigold, 210371
Trim: Benjamin Moore, Dove White OC-17

Mudroom
Walls: Morris & Co, Blackthorn, WM8610/1
Trim: Benjamin Moore, HC-7 Bryant Gold

Kitchen
Walls: Benjamin Moore, Dove White OC-17
Trim and Cabinets: Benjamin Moore, 1523 Embassy Green

Living Room
Walls: Benjamin Moore, 2144-30 Rosemary Sprig

Trim and Mantel: Benjamin Moore, 2144-10 Guacamole

Master Bathroom
Walls: Scalamandre, Sigfrid, WSB 0046 0425
Trim: Benjamin Moore, AF-545 Solitude

Master Bedroom
Walls: Philip Jeffries, 3367, Erics Ecru
Trim, Cabinets, and Mantel: Benjamin Moore, 1636 Providence Blue

Kid's Bath
Walls: Benjamin Moore, Dove White OC-17
Trim: Benjamin Moore, HC-159 Philipsburg Blue

Boys Bedroom:
Walls: Benjamin Moore, AF-545 Solitude
Trim: Benjamin Moore, HC-159 Philipsburg Blue

Girls Room:
Walls: Benjamin Moore, 2092-70 Fairest Pink
Trim: Benjamin Moore, 2092-60 Georgia Pink

Girls Bath:
Walls: Benjamin Moore, 2092-70 Fairest Pink
Trim: Benjamin Moore, 2092-70 Fairest Pink

Chapter 7: Whitland Avenue

Living Room
Walls: Farrow and Ball Tented Stripe ST1372
Trim: Benjamin Moore, OC-17 White Dove

Wet Bar
Walls and Cabinets: Benjamin Moore, OC-17 White Dove

Dining Room
Upper Walls: Benjamin Moore, OC-17 White Dove

Library
Walls, Trim, and Ceiling: Benjamin Moore, 712 Fort Pierce Green

Breakfast Room
Walls: Thaibut, Corneila T72604, Grey and Gold
Trim: Benjamin Moore, 1098 Toasted Almond

Vestibule
Walls and Trim: Benjamin Moore, 1098 Toasted Almond

Kitchen, Scullery, and Keeping Room

Walls and Cabinets: Benjamin Moore, 508 Tree Moss

Primary Bedroom and Bath
Walls, Trim, and Cabinets: Benjamin Moore, OC-17 White Dove

Powder Room
Walls: Sandberg Sigfrid Blue WSB 0046 0425
Trim: Benjamin Moore, OC-17 White Dove

Laundry Room
Walls: Morris & Co, Fruit, Beige Gold Coral, 216859
Cabinets and Trim: Benjamin Moore, OC-17 White Dove

Teen Loft
Walls: Stroheim 75003W Edie-05 Plum
Cabinets and Trim: Sherwin Williams SW 6499 Stream

Chapter 8: Parmer Avenue

Entry
Walls: Morris and Co Willow Bough, 216480 Green
Trim: Benjamin Moore, SW 7533 Khaki Shade

Keeping Room and Kitchen
Walls: Benjamin Moore, OC-44 Misty Air
Cabinets and Trim: Benjamin Moore, SW 7533 Khaki Shade

Dining Room
Walls: Schumacher Lansdowne Stripe, Limestone, 5004621
Cabinets and Trim: Benjamin Moore, SW 7533 Khaki Shade

Laundry Room
Upper Walls: Schumacher Santa Barbara Ikat, Neutral, 5009222
Lower Walls, Trim, and Cabinets: Benjamin Moore, 2138-50 Misted Green

Powder Bath
Walls: Cowtan and Tout, 20466-04, Tabor Teak

Butler's Pantry
Walls: Les Indiennes 156 Japanese Tree, Olive
Trim: Benjamin Moore, 2144-10 Guacamole

Evening Room
Walls, Trim, and Cabinets: Benjamin Moore, 2144-10 Guacamole
Ceiling: Phillip Jeffries 5286 Bermuda Hemp

Primary Bedroom
Walls: Phillip Jeffries 3365 Grass Roots, World Class White

Trim: Sherwin Williams SW 6229 Temple Star

Stair
Walls: Morris and Co Willow Bough, 216480 Green
Trim: Benjamin Moore, SW 7533 Khaki Shade

Primary Bath
Upper Walls: Benjamin Moore, OC-44 Misty Air
Lower Walls, Cabinets, and Trim: Benjamin Moore, SW 7533 Khaki Shade

Guest Bedroom
Walls: Schumacher 5004132 Willow Leaf Aqua
Trim: Benjamin Moore, SW 7533 Khaki Shade

Guest Bath
Walls: Benjamin Moore, OC-44 Misty Air
Trim and Cabinets: Benjamin Moore, SW 7533 Khaki Shade

Chapter 9: Smith Lake

Kitchen
Walls: Benjamin Moore, OC-44 Misty Air
Cabinets and Trim: Benjamin Moore, SW 7533 Khaki Shade

Family Room
Walls: Benjamin Moore, 2143-20 Alligator Green
Cabinets and Trim: Benjamin Moore, 2143-10 Sage

Bathroom
Walls: Benjamin Moore, OC-44 Misty Air
Trim: Benjamin Moore, SW 7533 Khaki Shade

Guest Bedroom
Walls: Scalamandre Estelle WSB 0076 0826 Dark Blue
Trim: Benjamin Moore, 2143-10 Sage

Bunkroom
Bunks: Benjamin Moore, SW 7533 Khaki Shade
Ceiling: Scalamandre WHN 000AP1003

Laundry
Upper Walls: Scalamandre, Karolina, Green WSB 00380807
Trim and Lower Walls: Benjamin Moore, SW 7533 Khaki Shade

ABOUT THE AUTHOR

Acclaimed interior designer Stephanie Sabbe is one of the country's most celebrated design talents. Named a *House Beautiful* "Next Wave" Designer and *Traditional Home*'s "New Trad," she has been featured in *Veranda, Southern Living, The Wall Street Journal*, and many more. When not in her Nashville design studio, Stephanie is chasing her four kids—Remi, Wells, Georgie, and Cora—or giving a hard time to her husband of eighteen years, Bryan. You can find her at her design shop, Heirloom Artifacts, or on Instagram @sabbeinteriordesign.